I0631745

LAST CALL:

The Bukowski Legacy Continues

Edited by RD Armstrong

© 2011 by LUMMOX Press
LAST CALL: The Bukowski Legacy Continues
Edited by RD Armstrong
All Rights Reserved

ISBN 978-1-929878-86-4

No part of this book may be reproduced without written permission of LUMMOX Press, except in the case of written reviews.

First Edition

The LUMMOX Press
POB 5301
San Pedro, CA 90733-5301
www.lummoxpress.com

Some of these writings have appeared previously in other magazines; the editor thanks them for their vision. Henry Denander's illustrations have been used in *The Bukowski Review, Cerberus* & *Microbe*. RD Armstrong's **"Last Stop"** has been published in *The San Pedro Poems* & *Fire and Rain Vol. 1*. Jay Alamares' **"Death Dirge in b-Flat"** appeared in *Last Call: A Legacy of Madness*. **Bukowski and the Romantic Influence** by Alex Thiltges is excerpted from his PHD thesis (that's *DOCTOR* Thiltges, now). **2 Drink Minimum** was originally published in *El Pagano and Other Twisted Tales*.

Last Call

LAST CALL:
The Bukowski Legacy Continues

FICTION

ESSAYS

INTRODUCTION

IN AN ODD TWIST OF FATE I have been mistaken for a longtime chum of the Buk (which, in this case, rhymes with duke), which is not true (except that I have read him almost my entire life). I've also been accused of being a minor Buk imitator by one side of the fence, while the other side marveled that I could be so inspired by him and yet still write a halfway-decent poem!

Many people have gotten a good run off their 'personal' relationship with him, hanging out, drinking beer and shooting the shit. I did not know that man, nor, to be honest, did I want to. The Buk I knew was the writer, the man whose ideals came through loud and clear in the character of Chinaski. That other Bukowski that some people knew looked, to an outsider like me, like just another drunken asshole. I had heard the stories, I had seen the films.

I grew up with him, but I didn't live in his neighborhood unless you count L.A. County. He was not a childhood buddy. It was his poetry (mostly) and his stories that I read from my 20s into my 50s. Four decades of Buk...a powerful tool to shape one's life, maybe, or just some damn fine material to read while waiting for the next bus to somewhere came along. The Buk was my diet for poetry, for most of those years, dominating Rilke, Ferlinghetti, Ginsberg and even Bob Dylan and Leonard Cohen (who wrote a very different kind of poetry). Even my namesake, the man who introduced me to "rain dog", Tom Waits, even his poetry was eclipsed by the Buk. Granted, Tom has the theatrical thing wired, but that just embellishes his talent... Buk never needed embellishment, in my humble opinion.

I became aware of the 'Dirty Old Man' in '68 or '69. I was a greenhorn. Just out on my own for the first time, with some pretentious ideas and the pictures that Buk painted sounded vaguely familiar to a

1

rebellious lad like myself. I thought I'd like to be like that when I grew up (*until I grew up like that and didn't like it much at all*)...

Even though I read Buk for years, almost up to the time of his death, it took me a long time to make sense of him. Before that, I had just been studying...not *learning*. Coincidentally, it was around this same time (the early '90s) that I also began to write in a 'voice' that made sense to me. So, although I studied Buk for a long time, I came late to this writing of THE POEM. Perhaps this is why I focus so much on the *words* of the man, and so little on his deeds (or those of his minions).

A lot of people don't understand the premise of this book (or the preceding version). They want to know why there isn't any Bukowski in a book about Bukowski. Well, that's just it...it isn't about the *legendary* Bukowski, it's about the influence of Bukowski on a generation of writers who followed him into the trenches to write in their own particular style. Before Bukowski became the legendary Bukowski, when he was just another schmuck writing the not-so-great American novel, when he had a snowball's chance in hell of catching a break, he was like some of you; living with his dreams and enjoying the fruits of his low-life, with no discernible future, hand to mouth, paycheck to paycheck...the writing more of a distraction than a way out. I'm sure that some of you readers know exactly what I'm talking about (I can't be the only one left who hasn't been sucked into the great American Myth machine).

Maybe it's our love of the underdog that makes us hold his miserable life up and celebrate it as if it was a beacon. He was the long shot who defied the odds and made it out alive. Every generation needs one, the oddball who manages to give the goon squad the slip; or the two-time loser who finally wins. But, really, that's all just publicity to forward the career, isn't it? The fans of Bukowski seem to love his laughable portrayal of the loser, the bum, the low man on the totem pole. The reality of all this is that he got out of his dead-end life as soon as he could, got a nice little house in San Pedro with a view of the harbor and a stones throw from a Catholic church up the hill.

Most of the Bukowski wannabees seem to think that if they can just emulate his supposed lifestyle (the boozing, skirt-chasing, freeloading, chauvinistic loner) they'll be on the fast track to fame and fortune! They forget that he endured all that for at least twenty-five years and emerged from it with a bleak cynicism that would take another ten years to mellow. But all this lost on those who just want to be the *legendary* Bukowski.

I'm not interested in becoming legendary...not that there's much chance of that happening. In reality, I have come to the realization that one has to be true to oneself; one has to follow their own path, even if the party is always on the other path. You have to be strong if you're to go it alone. Or you have to publish the occasional anthology that a lot of people want to be in. I think I'm somewhere in the middle.

So in this book I have attempted, *again*, to showcase a number of writers whose work shows the influence, not necessarily in style or form, but in the feelings that their pieces (especially true of poetry) provoke in the reader (or in the editor). Not too many reviewers ever address the visceral quality of Bukowski's writing, which seems odd to me since he was so fond of writing while listening to classical music, especially the darker stuff. It is music that tugs on one's feelings, pulling the dark undertones out and giving them a good shake. It is my opinion that Buk's poetry does the same.

Here's a good example of this in the poem, STYLE:

> *"Style is the answer to everything.*
> *A fresh way to approach a dull or dangerous thing*
> *To do a dull thing with style is preferable to doing a*
> *dangerous thing without it*
> *To do a dangerous thing with style is what I call art*
>
> *Bullfighting can be an art*
> *Boxing can be an art*
> *Loving can be an art*
> *Opening a can of sardines can be an art*
>
> *Style is the difference, a way of doing, a way of being done.*
> *Six herons standing quietly in a pool of water,*
> *or you walking out of the bathroom naked without seeing me."*

From **Mockingbird Wish Me Luck** *by Charles Bukowski*

This poem rolls along with what seems like the weight of the world riding on its back, as if the writer wants the reader to respond with a

3

heavy sigh as each point is made about this elusive thing called "style". And then, at the end, the twist: that style has something to do with the magic of ordinary moments…it's a beautiful and surprising moment.

This is the signature Bukowski poem for me. It captures everything within its twenty-seven lines. It is a neat little package. I wish that "mainstream" poets & scholars could see the utter simplicity of this piece. But it is lost in all the hype that surrounded the man.

His passing pushed me into the local limelight back in '94. I held a series of three memorials in his honor in San Pedro, California at Sacred Grounds Coffeehouse. It was there, while working as a dishwasher, that I saw him for the last time (the first being at the Sweetwater Reading in Redondo Beach, in 1980). He was old and frail and dying of Leukemia. I wrote the following poem about it:

Last Stop

The old guy sat at the table
with his wife
his back faced the room
a tuft of very white hair stood
on his head like a cloud
hovering close
over San Joaquin
farmland.

The old guy was about as big around
as a minute
his clothes hung loosely on his frame.
Perhaps they were not his clothes
but a gift from some well-meaning
patron-of-the-arts.
Maybe these were his clothes
and he was doing his best to fill them
with all that was left.

The old guy's wife smiled
and spoke to him in a low voice
inaudible to the rest of the room
her eyes twinkled
as he worked on a piece of cake

and sipped a cappuccino
his hands trembling.

As they left
she balanced his frail frame
against her own
he was going as fast as he could
and soon he would be gone
altogether.

Seeing Buk like that... well it just about broke my heart. It made me regret my being timid for all those years. Hindsight tells me now, that timid would not have faired well with the Buk. But then, I had only the impressions of one who had not put it together yet, one whose experiences were still solidifying. It would take another year or two for that process to begin (and still, it goes on today).

Buk brought the world into focus. Sure, there was adventure, but there was also an increased awareness of the pit falls and booby-traps that most of us must discover in life, and sometimes the lessons are learned the hard and painful way. Repeatedly. You could say that we both attended the School of Hard Knocks.

He confirmed that HUMANITY (if given half a chance) would always exceed well beyond one's *lowest* expectations.

This was his appeal to me; his cynicism. It cut through the bullshit of life's pretense like a laser through case-hardened steel and took the edge off the little nicks and scrapes that you can't avoid as you stumble down the path.

His work forms a significant portion of the foundation of my own technique, but it still is only a part of my own cosmology. A foundation without a structure on it is just a slab. Buk's work is a part of the skeleton on which we strive to hang our layers of experience, building the body of modern poetry; always striving for a more perfect design and *always* thwarted by our own frailties, our own human-*ness*. It is the strength of his work that rolls on, like an errant hubcap, released and hurtling towards the horizon, inspiring us to follow.

I'm certain the man I connected with back in the early seventies was more of a creation in my mind...an interpretation of Bukowski, more fictitious, than factual. Just as Buk interpreted his past to create Chinaski...he also re-created himself. It was the spirit or essence of the man that I was drawn to and the essence was strongest and most viable in his writing.

Each of us, at some point in our lives, must let go of a person who has been a mentor. We usually outgrow them. Sometimes they move on. Eventually there is death. Such is the case with Buk and I. Even though he died in 1994, his words and his memory have lingered. Many bitter things have happened since his death, things that have tarnished the memory of his greatness. In my own small way, I have attempted to honor his memory by not succumbing to the lure of an easy nostalgia. It is quite fashionable these days to laud the antics of the "Chinaski" persona while forgetting the *essence* of the Bukowski poem or short story.

After over forty years of reading the Buk, my opinion hasn't changed.

—RD Armstrong

Portions of this essay were delivered as a speech to the **Second International Charles Bukowski Symposium** *held in San Pedro in August of 2000 and later an excerpt from this essay was published in* **The Bukowski Review #3** *2004.*

ABOUT THIS BOOK

This version is a reinterpretation of its predecessor, *LAST CALL: The Legacy of Charles Bukowski.* In that version I attempted to show that Buk's writing & method of addressing the subject matter had influenced many writers beyond the "meat" school. I don't believe that I was as successful as I had hoped.

That said, in this new version, there is a broader scope of writing and I have been a harder editor to please. As one might expect, at the mere mention of Bukowski, there has been a tidal wave of response. But I have held fast to my definition of what is Bukowski-esque: namely writers of the "solid, clean, and unpretentious line" and not necessarily having to do with the Buk.

Some of the poems (as indicated by *) and most of the essays in this book are reprinted from the first version. Most of the stories are new.

POETRY

Claudio Parentela

C.C. Russell
A SIMPLE ANGER

What the voice said
across the horizon of dream
and what it meant
were separate, separated
by thought and useless deed.

Fuck polite desperation.

I will feed you the names
of the dead
until you are filled
with them

and gut you
from chin to cock
just to resurrect them
once more.

Pris Campbell
AT THE MERCY OF STONES

I am the woman
with stones in her mouth.
They crush weak protest
into slumbering whispers

Speechless,
between cold sheets,
I dream of old promises
and fragrant nights
once filled with hungry lovers.

The moon paints women
with strange eyes
and sharp fingers onto
my ceiling. They laugh
at my stubbed nails,
fallow breasts.

In shadowed blue visions, pages
part from worn bindings.
They drift out the window,
my story no longer.

Like Demosthenes,
I hope the stones teach
my tongue new stories
told in a fiercer voice.

(*Published in* Lotus Bloom Journal, Sept. 2003*;
In* The Women of the Web *print anthology, 2004
& it took First Place in the July 2003* PBL *competition.)*

G. Hagen-Hill
ANTIPHON (9TH AND PACIFIC)

Sirens and church bells;
Sunday morning anthem,
Jangle and clang,
Rhyme and discord.

The voice and drum of the harbor..
Rigging and wind,
Hangovers and hoodoo,
Sailors and hookers.

A tagger's indolent mark;
Silent trespass scrawled
On an old ship's soul,
Cat's eye accusation.

Yellow teeth chatter
Pious outrage!
Mumbled words filtered
Through dense cigar smoke.

Coffee, donuts, cops
Sprawl by the newspaper
Stand extolling
Yesterday's, Saturday's heartbreak.

In downtown doorways; self proclaimed
Redeemers confound and dismay, signify...
Mute believers stumble..
Outwitted-- public plowman.

Tempest is coming!
The dream is done!!
The end is near!!!
The trumpet is sounding!!!!

Chant, chant, chant,
Rat turds and crumbcakes;
Sweet Jesu, spirit gas,
Stale beer and urine.

A fitful communion
Beneath the bridge,
Across the harbor
In sight of golden

Mary, Star of the Sea
Her right arm extended--
In her left, a fishing boat cradled
Panis Angelicus among the garbage

And the flowers, perpetual misery..
Repent, repent, sad refrain...
Begs the question;
Begs the beholder,

What benevolent
Honorable world?
So much goat cheese
And spunk on street..,

Where's the prize?
What sanction?
What law? What phrase?
What sentence..

Up through the cracks
In the sidewalk
Springs green grass
From pagan bone meal

Buried beneath
Concrete and
Gravel bed.
Full vespers;

Filch a bit of space,
Dispatch feelers,
Following one seam
Or another.

Fat and fit from
The loins of squalor;
Almost swaggering
The great unnumbered

Linsey-woolsy parade
Life and death,
Hoist and heave
Forward.., a little at a time.
Gospel jazz that
Heats and swings....
Breathes spine
Back into a day.

Caught in an instant
Between the sirens
And the church bells
The wonder of God's puzzle.

Michael C. Ford
NOT CELEBRITY BOWLING:
CEREBRALLY BOWLING

spare me the hypocrisy with limitless sick
mortgages by white house fun-house monsters
in a shotgun marriage to the merry-go-round
of modern science.

spare me the hypocrisy of the pentagon goons
with their war-mongering phallic guided missiles
exploding all over the pudendum of the world.

spare me the hypocrisy of the literary elite: those
who conscientiously, with sinister energy really
do punish those language commando poets who
inherited integrity from their teacher-ancestors:
those who are continuously put on the crucible
for telling the truth too many times in public
recitations.

spare me the hypocrisy of the poetry contest: the
canonized college robots, insulated inside their
creative "typing" depts. rewarding the mendacious,
the malevolent, the mediocre.

spare me the hypocrisy of poetry slam idiot
ambitions: the jangle of the cash-register more
recognized and more rewarded than any honest
rebellion without payback, without a trade-off.

spare me the hypocrisy of the gutless rituals of
anthologized poetry; English Department ivory
tower cowards publishing what they have turned
the art of poetry into: bubbles on a fat vat full of
bland oatmeal.

spare me the cynical cinema garbage men
who in a conspiracy of ignorance pretend
John Cassavetes never existed and pander
to the lowest common denominator, making
splatter movies for 14-yearold mentality and
a plethora of reprehensible chick flicks for
the mass mess of enslaved audiences in the
media meat market.

Henry Denander
AT THE RACETRACK

On eBay I bought four whisky glasses from
Santa Anita Park; this was Charles Bukowski's
favorite race track and he spent a lot of time there.

I've never betted on the horses myself but there was
a race track close to our summer house in Sweden
and I went there when I was a kid.

I never really liked to watch the horses run but
I came to see my uncle Allan who was a
regular at the track. I liked him a lot and he
always gave me money for ice cream,
so even without betting I came out ahead.

And now, 45 years later, here I am
with my large Santa Anita whisky tumbler
with the engraved horses and jockeys,
a couple of ice cubes and a large splash
of Glenlivet whisky.

Maybe I'm slowly
beginning to understand
the art of horseracing
after all.

G. Murray Thomas
**TO THE EDITOR WHOSE NAME WILL APPEAR
ON MY NEXT REJECTION SLIP**

I sat up all night
drinking beer
and going over my
unpublished poems
searching for one written
in the cheap, Bukowski-imitation style
your magazine seems
to like so much.
At 5 a.m. I gave up
and wrote this one.

Ellaraine Lockie
POETS AT ANY PRICE

I tell you
Don't ever trust poets
They'll panhandle
prostitute, fake or take
to get at any truth

They'll exploit
confessor, friend or family
Confiscate the unconditional
Then give it back
smudged in black ink

I tell you
Because I've been truth's victim
Verbal accounts reiterated
verbatim in someone else's poem
Secrets exposed as sonnets
Composites as transparent
as the silk panties I wore

I tell you
Revere the poets' need
to reveal these small realities
Because bigger ones they bare
Bloody ones whitewashed by other informants
Journalists whose jobs are contingent on asking
easy questions at presidential press conferences

The partial truths that smell better
in perfume-sampled magazines
That taste better even as FDA-approved
poisons eat immune systems
That feel better because a cheating
spouse's arms are safer than none at all

I tell you
Don't ever trust poets
If you prefer deception
Because truth is their drug
And they'll do anything
for a fix

Previously published in the LUMMOX Journal

Louise Webb

Rebecca Morrison
BELL

Lupe makes cakes.

She rises before dawn
every day
and drives away
to bake.

Somewhere the
morning is filled
with sweet dough
and warm rolls.

Nana waits for
her on the porch
by the cactus.

She takes me by the
hand and says,
"This bloomed once
20 years ago and
I called everyone
in the middle
of the night."

I can see the century
plant flowering in
darkness as the
women pour
onto the streets
like summer heat.

Bell waits inside.
"This is Bell,"
she says.
He smiles.

She has waited
half a century
for him to
speak. Bell smiles

in the afternoon,
silver chimes ring
in the warm wind.

Somewhere, someone
has forgotten
the sun.

And somewhere else,
someone has picked
it up again,

wearing it like
jalapena red dangling
from her trellis

and deep mint ivy
twining round her fence,
twisting upwards.

4-18-04

Frank Reardon
SET YOUR IDOLS
ON FIRE

when
the ticks &
jitters
try to
become
one

they rub
together
like
"red phosphorus"
& sulfur,

igniting
one lonely
flame
inside
the dark
hand
of who i
am,

it is
the only
way

to
shorten
the lines
& remove
the
lies,

it is
the only
way
to set
the idols
on
fire,

it is
the only
way
to free
insanity
from
desire.

RD Armstrong
A WORKING MAN'S LIBRARY

Long before I ever
Knew I could write
Anything worth a damn
I began my library of all things Buk

Now it's forty years
Later and I am selling
It off to pay the rent

I thought I would be
Happy to be rid of
The books that I no
Longer read
Their usefulness and
Purpose long since
Forgotten
Just some stuff I
Drag around out of
Habit

But I feel lost
As if I have sold
My children into slavery

And for what?
A few hundred dollars
And forty inches of
Shelf space

(Published in E/OR – Living Amongst the Mangled*)*

Andrew Hilbert
SMOKE FOLLOWS BEAUTY

To hazel eyed Americana,
My bipolar disorder sweetheart,
Indian reservation beauty queen,
Star of the cigarette ashtray misery,
You're the cocaine angel.
This, my night watching epiphany:

Her eternal smile
Begins to fade.

(Originally published in Chiron Review*)*

Mende Smith
LINDA LEE

She is smaller now than my daughter is at fourteen
the golden freckles in her eyes spell "Hank"
and for her years, her own light shines brightly
left of center to the big writing man with scars on his face
there are so many questions in my glass of red wine
with this glass of red she insisted to buy me
so I drink slowly from the Bukowski Estate
and I listen to her voice through the ice cubes melting
and the loud music pushes up against her
through the windows from the inside of the bar
a party of five at an outside table
we two drinkers sip our drinks, and three sobers sip their coffee
speaking softly while the last lover speaks
and she is easily distracted but inveigle; wide eyes flashing
I ask her what it was like to wake up in that bed every morning
and she says "I like cats, and Hank did too."
she pours out his memory and knocks back seltzer and vodka and lime
spinning her plastic straw into her ice cubes, she smiles
"Now eight, no nine cats sleep beside me on Hank's side of the bed."
her eyes go wide to accent her joy and she looks like she might fit
        in a doll house
she says she just fed them and they kept coming and staying there
they loaf around the sunny windows of her San Pedro bungalow
four on the couch, two at the windows, the rest like chess pieces
        all over the floor
but she says that one of them only greets her in the morning
and no one else has ever seen that cat

she laughs at that mysterious cat and she tells its story
perched on the edge of her seat like a mystic she taps her teeth
on the rim of her glass in the rests between her words
when people come over it splits, it only knows her she says
and when it meows she says it sounds like "mama".
Which is what Hank called her and right as she said that
the music hushed from inside the bar and just for a minute.
just a drum beat, I could see those eyes shining
like they shined at Hank, plain and subtle and beautiful
there she was, Hank's woman. As she was to him, and nobody else
Immortalized, transcending outside of a thousand lines
"like mama," she says again this time, in a cat's little voice
she smiles again and then she looks away and I can
see the spark she lit in a poet that wrote down
so that the rest of the world could see,
and now she mystifies me

(published in How Dirty Girls Get Clean*)*

Michael Adams
ONE WOODY GUTHRIE SONG

Talking with my friend Phil
about the state of the world –
bad and only getting worse,
all of us rushing headlong
into the flames, ranting,
flailing at shadows.

I tell him about an interview I just
read with Gary Snyder – now 80 –
old wise bard, scholar and mountain climber.
Gary said towards the end that the state
of the world is dire and sometimes the only
thing that works is laughter.

Our dear old friend Dolores,
who lived her life ringed by mountains,
would say when we started to discuss
the Big Issues, like saving the world,
that it's hopeless, so let's all
chant, and sing, and dance.

Phil relates how the deep ecologists would sometimes
talk and talk until all that was left to do
was tell jokes,

Says that's all
that matters, that
and making music.
Phil is in his mid-60s
and is learning to play his first
musical instrument ever, the guitar.

He tells me, I want to be able to play one
Woody Guthrie song before I die.

Ben Smith
POETRY MONEY

She puts her hand around
my neck
in the morning
after my first reading
and says

I'm going to kill you
for your poetry
money

I tell her I lost the money
Before we made it home, anyway.

She smiles and
beats me off under the
blankets.

I better get in the
shower and out
of this bed or I'll
never get out
of this room
alive.

I heard Praying Mantis
eat their mates after making love;

God knows what they do
to a hung over poet,
after a hand job

Mark Terrill
BUKOWSKI: 3/10/94

I was sitting at my desk
working on a poem
when my wife came in
with the news
"Bukowski died"
I put down my pen
and leaned back
remembering how I
used to read his column
"Notes of a Dirty Old Man"
in the *L.A. Free Press*
long before anybody had
ever even heard of Bukowski
and how I once saw his face
that gnarly freakish thing
on the cover of a book
not knowing who it was
and picked it up
just for that reason
only to discover
it was the same guy
whose column I'd been
reading all those years
and there in those pages
was a world not unlike
my own, that same constellation
of booze, broads and despair
and I figured if he could do it
I could do it too
so I bought a second-hand typer
started writing poems and
sending them around
got published in *Vagabond*
along with Bukowski

a simple little thing
about the fifty-cent movies
but the point of the matter is
I probably never would have
written a single fucking poem
if it wasn't for that guy

More than anyone else
he proved that poetry
didn't have to be an
academic thing, or
strictly for sissies
or phonetic windbags
that it was something
that could be lived
and felt and understood
as real as that cheap red wine
as real as those bills
piled up in the mailbox
as real as that landlady
hounding you for the rent
as real as those shit jobs
and crazy fucked up women
as real as hangovers and
the blazing Los Angeles sun
as real as anything at all
Then I let that feeling
that had been lurking inside me
for the last couple of days,
as if I'd somehow *known*,
come up over me and
culminate in my chest
accompanied by a long, hard
lump in my throat and a
certain sogginess of the eyes
surprising even myself
And then that sudden acknowledgment

of irreplaceable loss that
came hammering down
When all the good people are gone
who will be left?
But why all these feelings
of tenderness and sorrow
for some pock-marked old geezer
who wrote dirty books laden
with great existential insights
whom I never even met?
Then it became apparent

In a frightening sort of way
that there are the
Great Living Poets
the Great Dead Poets
and then there's me
another two-bit guttersnipe
with a word-processor
and literary ambitions
of the burning kind
forever in debt to
a dirty old man
whom I never even knew
and I leaned forward
picked up my pen
and went back to work.

There's so much to do.

Buk, we'll miss you
like a son of a bitch.

(Originally published in Ends & Beginnings,
City Lights Review #6, 1994,
edited by Lawrence Ferlinghetti)

Doug Holder
IT IS LATE AND THE FRUIT IS BAD.

It is late at night
and the fruit
has gone bad.
Its bruises remind me
of all of life's hamfists
and the things
I never had.

I take its flesh
deep into my mouth
digest the ferment
of its rotten skin
cut the lights
in respect
for the state I'm in.

H. Lamar Thomas
LEAVING OFF WHERE MOZART ENDS

Is there anything here that I can spare? When the time comes to run
And the straight pine bends with the snow and the rain, with wind and winter
Will I have the balls to drive into Oklahoma hail storms and Texas boredom?
All I ever knew sits and waits, I try to wake her, all snores and night gas,
She sits dust caked while I wonder what would happen if I turn
The Janacek Dances up way up past what the yard is capable of muffling
And concealing, like why silence the mighty chords, the spit in the eye,
It strikes and it's down beat down beat devil's triad, and I'm smiling dancing.
What is *worth*, what am I leaving, and when the towers collapse
On my house and gardens it's better to chase the sunlight out and lock down
The curtains, race on, race away, gotta change this pace and face today.
Sometimes things just look a lot better when I am leaving,
Leaving this stupid permanence fixation, cranking the truck up,
Little red truck, Chevy darling and half a tank of gas,
Just enough to kick the stones off my ass and just enough to drive to tomorrow.
Buk tried to leave his palm trees and desert winds, his noisy corner
Of the LA purgatory, but he never had it so good that waking up never hurt.

Charles Ries
CAROLE MASO'S MASTER CLASS:
POET 0 / MONKEY 1

Master Class
Spa for the wordless

The men didn't show up
Just me and sixteen women
No sissies
          Earth goddesses and amazons
From what I could tell

Real men don't write narrative poetry
          in Milwaukee
Where's Charles Bukowski when you need him?

We take our turns
She encourages
          gently prodding,
"Tear down the narrative walls"
"Chase the monkeys from your mind"
"That's good -
          another 500 pages and you'll have a novel"
We laugh - we sigh - we cry.

"When your soul sings
Your words dance."

Maybe hers do....
Mine are all flat footed today.

I leave exhausted
The monkey wasn't obeying
So I invited him to lunch
Know thy enemy - win the war
"BLT for me and a banana for my friend with the pen."

John Dorsey
DOCTOR BUKOWSKI'S MONSTER
for abigail

in the sunlight of madness
bukowski's monster
has been turned into
the shadow of a young james dean

the meaning gets lost
caught up in the moment
where stanzas get tattooed
into the golden forearms
of nelson algren's over medicated grandchildren
searching for cool
with a broken flashlight
beamed toward karma

there is a junky born
every minute

read the label
shoot dice
ask questions later
ask the dust for its last dime
spit words at the sun
an eternal hot walker
wait for the photo finish
become a split second god
in another man's miracle

a house on fire
we came here to watch the words burn
golden like shelley's sperm
like cassius clay's draft card
like the embers of johnny cash's
last folsom cigarette

like the senseless dying of the light
we were built to rage against

like freedom fighters
searching for a match

in the rain

Henry Denander

Father Luke
THE CONTENDER

There is a pain so full
that the rest of it doesn't matter.
It forms rings in your body
through the years, like the rings of a tree.
The wrinkles on your face,
which should be happy
reminders of laughs,
are instead a travel log
of sorrow, and of sadness, and of pain.
It's no use saying no to the years.
Fighting time is like wrestling with the air.
No isn't the answer.
And neither is yes.
There aren't any answers.
There are only the years, which
look at you from the other side of the room.

Jay Alamares
DEATH DIRGE IN B-FLAT

I see it in Picasso's
"Guernica"
as it screams
silently at me
above the doorway
in grays
and blacks
and whites

I taste it in
the
air...
Los Angeles
air
bitter...
greasy...
and weary of
being
the air
for obvious reasons
and
those still obscure

I feel it in
the moon
which has forsaken us
in its
orbit
i avoid it
in the mirror
at all costs

I see it in
the concrete
which doesn't care...
which never cared
as it
strangles the flower
in the empty lot

I hear it
in the
screams from the
little girl's bedroom
as her drunken father
rolls her on her belly
whispers
"I love you"
and slides it
in
oblivious to her
screams

she has gone
insane months ago
at the age of 10

I hear it in the
sighs of the world
which buckles from the weight
of humanity...
unable to
sink
in the
vacuum
of space...
there's nowhere
to sink to

time ran out on us
long ago

our luck
is on
it's heels

(originally published in Last Call: A Legacy
of Madness – *VHP 1994)*

Michael N. Thompson
BLAME BUKOWSKI

If you don't like
How I observe the landscape
Like conspiracy theorists
Watch Zapruder's film
Or how I sink my fangs
Into the scars
Of downtown curbs,
Blame Bukowski

If you're opposed
To the way
I use my words
In the same manner
Van Gogh used watercolors
Or how I expose
The line between
Human and animal,
Blame Bukowski

If you disagree
With the reasons
I bow down
To the verse
Like a bull
About to face its matador
Or how I tear open
The assholes
Of literary backscratchers,
Blame Bukowski

Be forewarned though
If he were here now,
He'd tell you it isn't easy
To feel the fire
When you're used to
Plain portions

Bretton B. Holmes
EINSTEIN ISN'T SO SEXY ANYMORE

I sit
listening to
Women
talk about how sexy Einstein is

and I point out the fact he's been
dead a good long while

Probably not so sexy anymore
The worms have most likely gnawed off
what little attraction he held

But,
they say they find him terribly attractive regardless
"We'd marry him for his mind"

I point out quietly
what first the worms likely went for

they sit silently
and I chuckle
about the state of the world
between us.

lam Rawkinrec
ELBOW SONGS

They storm by my window
inside late night tornadoes
spinning idea, image, and simile
that need only fine tuning
to be completely complete.

Stretching into the open window
I grab one and yank it in. It squirms
like a fish, an electric snake
twisting around me and my keyboard
squeezing into me the good poison
of obsession
to pound the words down

if my Muse is not mad at me. See
sometimes it's a twister of debris
and catching one yanks me out
the window, knocked unconscious
unable to get that music
from my mind to the finger tips

waking to find myself
covered with hangover
naked in the back alley
blasted with laughter
and feet carrying school books
stomping past me.

John Yamrus
BUKOWSKI'S PROPERTY

this poem
isn't mine these
thoughts aren't
mine these
sentences aren't
mine these
cadences
aren't
mine these
lines aren't
mine.

nothing
i do
or think
or write
is mine.
it's all filtered down
through you
Mr. Bukowski...

and i wish
you'd
come here
and
take it
back.

(From NEW AND SELECTED POEMS,
LUMMOX Press, 2008)

Michael Lefanto
FORTY SHORT

I couldn't come up with the forty
needed for her
to stay the night.
A warm body next to mine
would've been nice.
Dope poetry cigarettes
I had plenty of,
and there was a bottle of wine
in the fridge
bought for a Sunday dinner
with the kids that never happened
for one reason or another.

I watched her dress and leave.
She wasn't shy,
the way my wife used to be.
Standing there in bra,
wriggling into panties,
cigarette hanging from mouth
her telling me,
maybe next time,
if I call later in the night,
she'd be able to work something out.

But she was a whore a prostitute
and I the John,
and next time it would be someone else,
and I'd still be forty dollars short.

F. N. Wright
BUKOWSKI & ME

Like bukowski was
I am a beer
drinking machine

I think I am even
beginning to get
his great white
whale belly

I also like 1800
& jack daniels

crown royal
ain't bad either

also like bukowski
did do fuckin' well
I attract bad women

drunks
junkies
whores

thieving cunts
who will leave you
when someone else
with more money
or lies
to better feed their
addictions & habits
comes along

catholic girls gone bad
& baptist minister's
daughters
are particularly
fond of me

unlike bukowski
I am not
a great poet
but I'm damn good
sometimes

& as long as I can
tread water
the words will flow.

(Published in Bukowski and More, *2008)*

Gerald Nicosia
FOURTH OF JULY WITH THE BUK IN SAN PEDRO

He stands in a cheap plaid shirt
like some long-forgotten comedian
eyeing me sidewise
wondering what I want out of him
amazed that he's still alive
after 70 years of people coming at him
pleased by the magic he's still got
that keeps making books upstairs
on his little Mac computer
with the ancient radio blaring
the best classical music
after a day at the track
in one of the best Jap cars
money can buy
so many people coming to visit
the millionaire writer
in his fancy home and lush green yard
with self-cleaning swimming pool
don't see the lonely, troubled man
still inside
70 years haven't blunted the pain
of getting out of bed every morning
with an ugly face and a treacherous body
the horror of boredom
and the ever-nearing grave
they want to make him a hero
of the lost and down-and-out
king of the losers
what a joke
losers don't have kings
and Buk almost stumbles and falls
into the outdoor cooking grill
with wife Linda rushing to save him
though he'd already gotten his balance back

despite the dozen beers already downed
he plays with it all
the joke of holidays
celebrating your nation's independence
when your nation never gave you anything
but a big kick in the ass
and most of all the guests he invited
unaware they're foils for his madness
his need to compose their needs and hopes
into story after story
using humanity like notes in a symphony
it makes him happier than booze
and he can't figure out why
life can still be this good
when it's also so awfully
awfully bad.

Michael Monfort

Joan Jobe Smith
ARETHA FRANKLIN, BABY, WITH RESPECT

Aretha Franklin, baby, am remembering you When.
Not that When when you wore that big hat at Obama's
Inauguration but the When of August, 1966, year after
the Watts Riots when I met you at that blacks-only club
on Crenshaw in Watts week before your "Respect" aired
all over the radio and got you rich, famous and respected.
They didn't know why white chick me was in the club,
that I'd been dumped by my sexpot go-go girlfriend
Linda Alura who'd taken off with her Black Panther
lover and I didn't even drink, just sat there on the floor
on those crash pillows, snapping my white chick fingers
to the soul sound beat as you, Aretha Franklin, baby,
sang your R-E-S-P-E-C-T spelling it the way it should be
loud and clear while that groovy black dude taught me
how to Bugaloo, Shingaling, Jerk and Temptation Walk.
Oh, baby, what a rough 1966 I had while you moved on
to a great future. My 1967 wasn't much better so when I
auditioned at the Condor Room up in North Beach, I
picked on the jukebox for irony and good luck your new
hit song Respect, just a little bit of respect I wanted, too,
in those days when just a gaudy go-go girl. I got the job
but turned it down, too scared to go topless, so came back
to L.A. go-go. And now, Aretha Franklin, baby, you're
not doing well; news of your illness got me remembering
you, though you'll never know how much I respect you,
remember every day your soul sound real and wise, your
black woman big heart, your finger-snappy upbeat always
got me going when it was my turn to dance, even when I
didn't want to--but always remembering how to spell
R-E-S-P-E-C-T right and proud when no one else did.

(Published in AMBIT - UK, *Aug 2011)*

Alan Catlin
IF THERE WAS AN

analogy for her life
it would be a 1990's
film noir screenplay
of a 1960's biker flick
called Madwomen in Miniskirts
and she would be
the main sleeze
so far gone in her
20's the phrase,
LIVE FAST DIE YOUNG
LEAVE A BEAUTIFUL CORPSE-
was already passé
when applied to her,
she had that look about
her of a backroom
artiste in black
stiletto heels,
mesh stockings
and a dominatrix
whips and chains
even standing still
leaning on a lamppost
smoking a cigarette
her mind was going
a thousand miles
an hour while her
right foot tapped out
some secret rhythm
of a bone palace ballet.

Éric Dejaeger
LEGS
For Buk

First warm day
in early spring
Women wearing
brand new short skirts
and freshly shaved white

legs   legs
legs   legs
legs   legs
legs   legs
legs   legs
legs   legs
legs   legs
legs   legs
legs   legs
legs   legs
legs   legs
legs   legs
legs   legs
legs   legs

Bill Gainer
MY FOURTH OF JULY IN IDAHO, 2011

They sell mortar size fireworks
for personal use
here.
People shoot them off
in their front yards.

On the Fourth
the sky is lit 360 degrees,
the noise makes it sound
like a war zone,
the smell of gunpowder
takes me back
to my youth.

The morning paper
is quick to report,
not a finger or eyeball
were lost,
no houses burned.

On the fifth
all that's left
is to pick up
the beer bottles
and figure out
whose car
is parked in your
driveway.

I love it.

A.D. Winans
SAN FRANCISCO INSOMNIA

Tossing turning
Praying for sleep
When all else fails me
But God has no time
For insomniacs
And Christ must be busy
Preparing for the resurrection

Falling asleep for an hour or two
Head churning buttermilk dreams
The Holy Ghost stops by for a chat
Seems like an amicable chap
Swaps stories from the past
Just as if he were one of the boys
As I gradually surrender to his will
Dreams lined-up like shots of tequila
At a Mexican brothel
Only to wake again and again
Insomnia a heavily armored
Spanish conquistador
Takes no prisoners
Plays your mind like a card shark
Your body like a whore
In the morning leaves you feeling
Like bits and pieces of a shipwreck
Washed up along the shore

Doug Draime
SMALL HOUSE ON WINNONA BOULEVARD
August 1976

it's nothing much:
a large hole in
the earth
with some kind
of reddish weed growing
they call a rug,
from the center of
    the floor.
there's a painting
        a friend
        painted of
        a sculptor,
        who's name
        escapes me
        on the wall.

there's my cat, Electra; a bed, 1 chair,
159 books; the tiny kitchen with a few
dishes, couple of pots and pans; the work table,
the typewriter and the rest; the
bathroom with green mildew spreading
in the shower stall.
it's in the back of the Mexican illegal's house,
on the corner next to the real estate office,
across from Shakey's Pizza , a few blocks from where
Charles Bukowski lives, who advises me in a poem
(though he doesn't know me from Adam),
to remain 'underground' till it's my time.
I walk by his court apartment
going to my job at the porno bookstore, and I salute
him from the darkness of Carlton Way. I
salute the famous poet of East Hollywood.

Lawrence Welsh
OBITUARY

from hollywood
i drove to the westside
ate lunch
then shot down stocker east
through south central
up martin luther king boulevard
jazz till 2 a.m.
and watched crossing
guards escort boys
and girls across the street
passed sunshine
bright
clear
the calling card lounge
the ski hut's
chain-locked door
the menlo room
closed since 1948
and the coliseum
cracked and beat
2 riots and 7 earthquakes
to figureoa
turned left and moved beyond
julie's trojan barrel
green light
red light
cachao and eddie palmieri
oscar 'd leon
and war
pumping through air
a black lincoln
cuts in front
booming bass
cruising
into downtown civic
center next to

beggar jack
the shoe shine boy
and the one-legged
wheelchair bound
vietnam veteran who
whispers good morning
every afternoon
subterranean park
up the stairs
sit and dial
974-2233
you have 1 message
press 1 to listen
press 2 to...
press
"hey lawrence
this is your brother sean
i don't know if you
heard
but they're saying
on the news that
bukowski's
dead"

(First appeared in The Wormwood Review, Vol. 34,
Number 1, Issue 133; *and in* Das Ist Alles: Charles
Bukowski Recollected, *Pearl Editions)*

Ed Jamieson Jr.
MOVIE

in the back row, alone, I like the back that's were you see it all
but the problem with the back row like any row
except for the very first row is that there's a row in front of your row
and that's what always causes problems and that's why I stay home and watch
TV
but then sometimes I like to get out and see what the world is up to and act
like I'm part of it
and sometimes I like going out and not going to a bar to get drunk sometimes
I like seeing life sober
and when I'm thinking this
and when I thought no one would sit in front because there were many empty
seats
a couple sat in front of me even though there were many empty spaces
and the man had a bag of popcorn and a soda and he started slurping
crunching yanking
the crunch slurp yank crunch crunch slurp slurp started to ring in my ears
I had enough I moved across to the other side still in the back row
then when the ringing stopped
then another couple sat in front of me, with a giant size bag of popcorn and
a super-duper size cup of soda crunch slurp yank crunch slurp yank crunch
slurp yank crunch slurp yank sharing their crunch slurp yank crunch slurp
yank crunch slurp yank crunch
they must have been married
I moved to the fourth closes row to the screen two seats down at ease
comfortable
then some guy came and sat behind me, he had no food and drink so I gave in
and stayed at my position
the lights dimmed the previews began and I closed my eyes praying this guy
behind me would stay quiet

after four or five previews of movies I won't see the movie started about a
writer who I liked who wrote down some good words
and all was quiet except for the sound of the movie
so I sat there listening and listening and listening to the writer whine
about his father beating him- what father didn't beat his son- I sat
listening about how his jobs were horrible- every paycheck to paycheck is
horrible- I sat there listening about his many loves- shit I thought at
least he had many- what was he whining about so they went on and on about
his hard life I've seen too many hardships to feel any pity for a writer who
had a retirement a steady allowance an inheritance so I sat there looking at
my watch waiting for the next movie to start in the theatre next to me
I think it was a comedy or a fantasy or a horror movie I can't remember

"an intellectual is a man who says a simple
thing in a difficult way: an artist is a man who
says a difficult thing in a simple way."

Joe Speer
MY COMRADES

this one teaches
that one lives with his mother and cat
another pencraft master takes drugs, non prescription
and cleans house as his wife earns a living
this graduate of writer's cramp
sleeps on couches, drinking beer and making his spiel
In 1469 Sir Thomas Malory wrote *Le Morte d'Arthur*
while in prison
a French ambassador paid Cervantes a visit in 1616
he expressed surprise to find the author of *Don Quixote*
"a gentleman, a soldier, and so poor"
the ambassador suggested such a man be subsidized
in 1849 Dostoevsky was arrested
charged with having a secret printing press
in 1851 Herman Melville's *Moby Dick*
was worth more melted down as lamp oil
than for any literary commercial clout
in 1871 Thomas Hardy published his first novel
at his own expense
in 1898 Emile Zola was prosecuted by the government
found guilty of libeling the army
friends smuggled him to England
in 1913 Marcel Proust published *Swann's Way*
at his own expense
censorship and allegations about his doubtful patriotism
forced D. H. Lawrence into expatriation
William Faulkner smuggled rum

on a speedboat in a Louisiana bayou
until his sound became a fury
In 1966 John Martin of Black Sparrow Press
came across a hard-drinking postal employee named Charles Bukowski
another post Buk transcriber hangs out in the public library
a poetic libertarian
another comes from a rich family, like Henry James
and does not touch
"the skin of the working people"
my comrades are everywhere
we are saving the world
one poem at a time

Joy Buckley
NOT BUKOWSKI

it was either a
fast track day
at hollywood park
or wet with the smart
money on the mudders
jim i said look over there
that's charles bukowski
in line up ahead of us
moving now toward
the clubhouse where
he would be lost from sight
until he reappeared with his
head bent over a racing form
penciling in the day's bets
maybe scribbling a poem
in the margins about ass-
holes who bothered him
while he was working on
his picks not me i thought
i am too cool for that
after the 5th waiting
in line for a chili dog
damn if he wasn't right
behind me what could
i do hello i said
his face was kind
but his eyes were sly
he raised his right hand
palm turned outward
i'm not him he said
he looked dead at me
& then he smiled
i'm not bukowski

Jayne Lyn Stahl
PASSIONATA

I awake to your smell
still familiar like
sweat on swollen testicles.
I awake to a face that no longer
belongs to you but to
memory your
childhood the last word in
the mouth of
a dying man   a pulse that
dares from
another dimension   passion
a landscape of
lovers refracted through
frozen glass like the sound gravity makes
when it shatters passionate as
brazen ghosts
never to be silenced again.

Rick Smith
WE'LL ALL GO TOGETHER

I'm there on a barstool
knocking them back
cold and in bottles
watching my reflection,
wondering how I'll go.

By thirst or hunger
ear splitting glass filled thunder
out on the East River Drive.
A slow silent growth
inside the chest,
an inferno over Kansas,
high in an otherwise untroubled sky.
Or a bullet to the head
when I walk into some mini-mart
in San Bernardino
for a damn Mars bar.

Or what if I trade it all
for something that shines,
something held up in the distance,
a gold certificate,
something wrapped in silver foil.

Later,
I walk a dirty sidewalk
where spit shines like diamonds
where neon lights the way.

I'm thinking,
we'll all go together,
it'll be over
in a moment.

William Taylor Jr.
POEM

the missing co-ed
is found dead
and the rent
is twelve days late
the milk has gone sour
and the sky is the color
of charcoal
and smells of
gasoline
heart disease
claims more lives
than cancer
these days
or maybe it's the
other way around
nobody knows how to
write a goddamned
song anymore
and the 21st century
was the dumbest thing
you ever bought
all the wars
you paid for are live
and in color
but the TV is broken
and the house,
the house is out of
whiskey again.

Edward Field
THE BUKOWSKI OPTION
in memoriam Charles Bukowski

An old guy has two choices:
      the Bukowski Option,
which allows you to express all your nastier impulses
      and tell the world to go fuck itself --
this is the Way of Purity, the Bohemian Ideal,
      with its vow never to Sell Out.
On the other hand, whether you sell out or don't,
      you can try, in your old age,
for the discipline of Dignity,
      which is made more difficult
      when you have to take a leak
and every restaurant has a sign in the window,
      "Toilet for customers only."

I lived most of my life as a freak
      which expressed my contempt
      for the capitalist system.
Eventually, though, I too opted for Dignity
      as a protection and disguise
for my battered dreams --
      ideals I still believe in.

But, I ask myself,
don't you want to be a rebel anymore,
      an example to youth?
Yes, but I'm too dismayed
      by that sagging face in the mirror
and too conceited
      to look like I have dirty underwear
or droopy pants like a full diaper.
      Even Buk didn't grow a beard,
which would at least have saved his five
      most wasted minutes of the day, shaving,
and even have covered the scars
      of acne, drink, and time.
But his beauty was
      that he insisted on thrusting
his entire ugly face in our faces,

which was tremendously entertaining, of course,
and he knew it,
even as he snarled at the world.

Can you take the Bukowski Option, I wonder,
and not turn into a wreck?
What would it be like, I wonder,
to live like a slob,
and smoke my head off, drink,
and eat junk food?
I'm too much of a hypochondriac.
But at some point, maybe,
when there's nothing left to lose?
As my mother always said,
When you need a drink, you need a drink.
That time, at least, has come --
frequently.

The Dignified Option would seem to mean
staying out of sight,
maybe retiring to the country,
except it's too boring,
especially with the old back
ruling out gardening.
A composer I knew, like the man without a face,
would only go out at night
to take long bus rides
through deserted neighborhoods.
What the hell was he supposed to do?
Dignity is a good way
of disappearing, then even in public
no one will notice you.
They're all just thankful the old wreck
isn't being a troublemaker.

But even as a Dignified Gent, it's a constant
struggle not to be nasty,
because you don't have to be Bukowski
to have a ball of hatred and disgust
in your gut for the world.
Though unlike him I'll admit
I'm a sucker for lovey-dovey people.

Still, I wonder about the pixyish codgers
with their wispy hair and illumined eyes,
        playing giggling Chinese sages
as if old age was a barrel of laughs.
        They've either found something I haven't,
or are frauds.
        I'd guess the latter.

I cringe when I think of that librarian, once,
        cooing at my shrunken, ancient father
and him twinkling back, playing her game. Pitiful!
        Nasty would be better,
like dropping a loud fart, for example,
        in the hush of the library.
The woman at the supermarket checkout counter
        who automatically makes two bags for me --
while I think I'm getting points for being Dignified,
        she knows all about old men's prostates,
however good an act I put on.
        Leaving a puddle on the floor
would be a satisfying slap in her face
        for reading me like a book,
and with the long walk home ahead, a relief,
        even with wet pants leg flapping.

My lament is this,
        that any dog anytime
is free to squat
        or lift its leg to pee,

and on the street Bukowski
        or any normal freak
would simply turn to a wall and take
        a necessary leak,

which sometimes makes it seem
        that my worst mistake
was choosing
        Dignity.

You win,
        Bukowski.

Gerald Locklin
A BLOSSOMING

On Easter Sunday morning
On my Sirius car radio
I heard a saxophonist playing "Blossom,"
And I knew that Sonny Rollins
Had to be the man, No one else
Pours every breath of every extended riff
Of every dance of every strophe into
The molecular complexity of life itself,
Including its response to the antistrophe
Of death. Losing ourselves in such resurrection-requiems,
We know that death does not succeed in cheating
Us of life, that Blake and Rollins-all of the anointed-
Intuited that Eternity and every Instant are inseparable.
Time is the greatest lie,
And Loss the worst illusion:
The grave, the funeral pyre, decomposition:
All are movements of a single symphony.
Someone strode out of that sepulcher.
He was smiling and his wounds were healed.
He was singing and he even felt that he might be allowed
A little swagger. There was laughter in his leap.

The longer sonny lives, the more of us he lives on in,
And the more he sounds like the sun.

(Published in Modest Aspirations *– LUMMOX Press, 2010)*

RD Armstrong
POETICS

Today in the checkout at Ralph's
The checker asks me
"Do you know Carlos Bukowski?"
Carlos I think?
I know a Charles Bukowski, why?
Please don't be insulted but
You remind me of him...

It's the week before the Buk's
Ninetieth birthday
Even though he died almost
Twenty years ago
And plans to celebrate the
Glory that is everything Buk
Happen in Los Feliz this
Saturday night in a party
For the Bukowski faithful
And I
The forgotten
One of his ardent fans
Is being confused
For the old goat down
Here in Long Beach...

Yeah
I told the checker
I get that a lot
Me and Buk
Go way back

That's cool
She says
As she gives me
A deal on the Jif
Peanut butter I just bought

At last
My association with
Bukowski
Is finally paying off

(Published in E/OR – Living Amongst the Mangled*)*

Isaac Edwards aka Todd Jackson
UNTITLED
(for John Thomas, Philomene Long and some guy they knew)

yeah,
I've been to San Pedro
and paid my respects.
I saw the bottle caps
from around the world
on his grave
and I smoked a J,
instead.
I'm not him, he's not
reincarnated.

I could give a fuck
about Charles Bukowski -
drunk ol' dead bastard

His writing, however, means
everything to me.

My original instructors of the pen
were
Philomene Long and her husband
"the strong man" John Thomas.
They taught me the art
of my own voice; the beauty
of precise words and descriptions.
They showed me the Madness
of Bukowski blended
in the Bathtub with the beats
and the world beyond -
my world. Again,
I could give a fuck
about Buk, but when I read
about Hank Chinaski
I believe in
the power of the written word
to help us understand
each other, and god willing,
ourselves.

Linda Lerner
VISIONS OF OUTLAW GHOSTS

they shoot their way out of death
in post offices   slip
thru cracks nobody sees widening
sees beneath masks
Billy the kid   Dillinger hiding out
in backalley art   whispering
to poets / bluesmen   comeback on
album covers and t-shirts
the skeleton with a rose between his teeth/

civil servants sorting/carrying
letters   parcels   cramming
them into holes

Bukowski   ten years with
a leather sack on his back
the worst routes because
he had a vocabulary
wouldn't bend under the stone
boss / Mr. Stone

would have killed someone every day
taken that pony express ride in
Denver New York New Jersey
post offices through out America
to deliver his message: another
disgruntled employee
holding dullness hostage

if he hadn't been a drifter
taken up squatter's rights
on the page
fired away when
the stone came down too hard
barely room even to breathe
hear the brothers calling to him
to whisper back:
deliver his life

Neeli Cherkovski
SHOSTAKOVICH CAME TO VISIT

way back then we'd gather, you and I
with Rachmaninoff, Sibelius, and Mahler,
they would rise out of a radio sitting on a side table
near the couch that smelled like a dead cat

you loved those guys, "tough old men"
as you once called them, the grave masters
who drew power out of chaos and despair
without the use of words

you used to say, "The human voice ruins
the music," as Mahler struck like thunder
in your De Longpre Street living room, I
remember how you'd grip your bottle of beer

to the gods of music, you knew their lives,
and talked of therm; one evening it was
Dimitri Shostakovich, one of the last
symphonies, it rained that night, you could

hear it, that L.A. rain, the kind that
never stops, it keeps on coming even
when you're old and gray, even as the
years vanish, but that night it was young

and we were glorious smoking cheap
cigars from Ned's Liquors, and the
Russian composer battled it out
with duels and death; "He's like

a God," you said, the music
pushing and pulling on us, and
then it was forty-two year later,
you were gone, the apartment

now a city landmark, in memory
of you, your typewriter, and
the radio, and I'm attending
an opening reception

in your honor at the Huntington
Library, the bartender hands
me a diet coke, I tell him,
"Bukowski and I used to drink beer

four days in a row while
listening to music," he
responds, "Who is
Bukowski?" then I

looked at the display cases
with your letters, manuscripts,
and books, and photographs
on the wall. . .

I didn't tell the bartender,
One night Shostakovich
came to visit us while we
drank to excess, he chain-

smoked and bit his nails,
but when the music began
he turned into a tower
of fire, we sat back and

drained our bottles. so
that was life back in 1969
more or less, now it's a bit
more tame, now you are

there in the library
with Chaucer and the one
you called Willy the Shake,
and Dimitri still sells, maybe

not like in the old days,
but times change and, I
imagine, so must the muse
and the music.

FICTION

Claudio Parentela

Jason Hardung
AMERICA THE BEAUTIFUL

AMERICA, MACEO'S EX, CALLED to ask if he would kill her. Maceo agreed, just to see how she would react. He knew she threw those words around when she was broke or lonely, or both, but would never go through with it. Things would eventually get better and she wouldn't need him anymore, until the next crisis. She was never one to take responsibility for her own life. Just like she expected a man to rescue her from herself, now she was expecting one to end it for her.

America was from the city of angels. America was pushing forty, but her features clung to her bones as if she was a solid twenty eight. She had the legs of a Rockette and lips that the Hollywood starlets blow fake kisses from. She smelled of peaches and had a heart-shaped birth mark where her real heart was. Some of her family abandoned her, some of them died. To make a bad situation worse, her new landlord, a suavacito in a pin striped suit, raised the rent on the place she had lived for years. She was about to be homeless-- her sad childhood pondered again.

Maceo explained how it would go down if in fact she was serious and she was to listen to his every command. She would fly to him, Colorado. Phase one: He would score the heroin. That was the easy part. Her blood pumped virgin platelets, it wouldn't take a heavy dose. She had never done anything stronger than party drugs. Drugs without names, only initials, produced by gloved hands in a sterile lab instead of the thick insected sweat of a third world country. But Maceo, his blood dirtied like a street corner had acquired the tolerance of an Irvine Welsh character. Phase two: they would park in somebody's garage and leave the motor on, the door closed. Preferably the garage of a person that didn't like him. He would rather piss someone off than disappoint them. The soundtrack of their last breath would be his choice-- *Blood On The Tracks.* Phase three: While the carbon monoxide filled the car he would inject her, and then himself. By the time the first chords to *You're Gonna Make Me Lonesome When You Go* were strummed they would be leaned back in the seats asleep. He had to keep at least one vein fresh, not poke it until that night, let it come back to the surface like an earth worm flushed out of soil by a storm. He hadn't time to waste finding a spot to hit. Death has the patience of a child. And besides, there wasn't a way in hell he wanted to be charged with murder when murder was a favor to the victim, this was the same as loaning someone a ten spot or picking a friend's kids up from school and being charged with kidnapping. Her being his ex it just wouldn't look right. They both had to die equally. He drafted this plan into a written contract believing she would change her mind and never sign it, or what he was really hoping for--she would fly out and he would have time to apologize and make things the way they once were.

America touched down at Denver International on a cool morning. Maceo was to pick her up at 8am. It was already half past and he had barely hit the highway. The Rockies to the west wore their clouded crown, where the great plains stopped and handed over the sword and the promised land pawed from behind like a cage full of angry tigers. Maceo noticed none of that as he stopped at Johnson's Corner, a mom and pop truck stop on I-25 known for its cinnamon rolls.

He sauntered through the restaurant towards the bathroom, an old women gnawing on her bread looked up at him, disgust drooping from her wrinkled face. "Can I help you darlin'?" a waitress asked. He smiled, "I need to use the restroom. Been driving for hours." She looked in his eyes, then down at his arms and walked off.

The bathroom hummed with fluorescence. Some truck driver had left a large shit in the toilet. Maceo covered his mouth and nose with his t-shirt, flushed, and saddled it backwards. He dug his works from a cargo pocket and laid a spoon, a syringe so old the numbers worn off, a tiny piece of tar wrapped in black plastic on the back of the tank. He reached over to turn on the water in the sink but nothing came out. The drug has to get in the blood, by any means necessary so he straightened the needle with his fingers, lowered it into the toilet and drew water from the bowl. People are not china dolls, hard and shiny, they come softly--parts malleable. The only thing ever in the way of anything is a few layers of skin.

There was a knock on the door. "Is everything ok in there?" It was the waitress.

"Yes ma'am everything is fine. Had the shits since New Mexico." Maceo lied as he desperately tried to find a vein.

"Other people might need to use the restroom you know. You ain't even ordered nothing."

"God dammit, I haven't, I mean "ain't" ordered nothing because I'm trying to take a shit. Ok? How am I supposed to put new food in my stomach if I can't get rid of the old stuff?"

The waitress stomped back to the kitchen. Maceo finally hit a vein, packed up his gear and opened the door, a spot of blood staining his shirt sleeve. Silverware beat off porcelain, the scent of cinnamon and conversation filled the room—a white noise not unlike the sea rushing ashore, the rain against a window or insects mating in the dark. It seemed as if the whole joint was staring at him, the cooks, the truckers with silver dollar eyes and unshaven jowls, the old lady still trying to chew her bread, and especially the waitress. He noticed none of it walking through like Henry VIII himself was on his throne ready to knight him.

America was waiting on the curb with her luggage, smoking, legs crossed looking at a watch that wasn't there. An omnipotent voice on the loudspeaker announced it was code orange, it was always code orange, Maceo thought. He scratched his face. She looked the opposite of opaque sitting there, So Cal tanned in the crowd of pale hurried faces. She had the ocean in her hair and a scowl on her face. The urge to kiss her was there, but he didn't succumb. "How was the flight?" he asked. She didn't say anything as he lifted her bag into the back seat.

"You look mad," Maceo said.

"Well it is ten o' clock. I'm already stressed enough and you decide to show up two hours late."

"It wasn't a conscience decision. I got tied up in traffic. What's time anyway, when we are about to be eternal?" grinned Maceo.

She shook her head in disgust. "I don't want to talk about that right now. I feel jet lagged. Let's get something to drink before we get back on the road." He rubbed the back of her neck as they pulled off, she slapped his hand away. "Why can't you keep your eyes open?" she asked.

"Just tired," he answered.

It was a few days earlier-- vinegar scented liquid boiled as the cat rubbed figure eights around Maceo's legs. He said, "I love you," to it and pet it before he ripped the filter off a Marlboro, rolled it in a ball with his finger tips and delicately placed it in the spoon. Immediately, it absorbed the rank water. He pulled the plunger back with his thumb until the cotton was vacuumed white again. The syringe tip flashed against the blue television light as he traced a vein collapsed along his bicep. The phone rang. It was his mother, crying, trying to catch her breath. "You need to be honest with me right now. Please be honest with me." Now, more than anything he wanted to slam the heroin. He reverted back into that shameful little boy when his mom cried. When any woman cried.

"What the hell is wrong? Why are you crying?" he asked, still hunting a vein.

"Macey is everything alright? You aren't thinking of doing something stupid are you?"

"Mom, I'm always thinking of doing something stupid. That doesn't mean I'll do it. Why do you care now? What the hell are you getting at?"

"You aren't thinking of killing yourself are you?"

Maceo swallowed hard then forced a laugh, setting the syringe on the table. "No, mom. I'm not thinking of killing myself. How come all of the sudden, 10:30 in the morning you think that? People kill themselves after dark."

"I had a strong premonition. It's only happened one time before." His mom was not a spiritual person. The only time she ever mentioned God was when she was cursing him.

"Well, did that premonition turn out true?"

"Yes."

Maceo stood up and gazed out the window, not really looking at anything, but there were cars out there and some people getting into those cars and the sun was almost warm on his face. "And what was that one about?" he asked.

"I had a premonition that your sister Lizzy was going to get married. A real strong feeling in my heart. The next day she called from Louisville and just like I predicted-- told me she was engaged."

Maceo exhaled, "I hate to tell you this mom, but I'm not planning on killing myself. And anyway, it wasn't a big secret that she would get married someday. She's been with that loser for seven years."

The crying slowed. "Just know my life would be ruined if I lost you. I know I wasn't the best mom--"

Maceo interrupted, "Here we go. Just stop. You did the best you could at the time. I mean when you were around. My fucked up life isn't always your fault. I'm not going to blow my brains out. I promise. And if I do decide to, you'll be the first person I call. Now, I've got to go. I'm late for a meeting or something."

"Please be careful Maceo. I love you."

He hung up the phone and picked up the loaded syringe. It made a popping noise as it broke through scar tissue.

What his mom said bothered him. If she only knew. Lying back on the pillow, eyes focused on the wilted prayer plant hanging from the ceiling, he imagined: what the gun barrel tasted like-- how all that fire power would feel when it shook his teeth, his tonsils, that pink flap of skin in the back of the throat, blowing out the brain from the back of the skull like beautiful red confetti as the clock strikes a new year. Would he be in pain or would heaven open up just past the popcorn ceiling? Could he look down while floating upward on broken wings and watch paramedics tend to his limp body? Would the pillow behind his head soften the bang? Or worse yet, what if he lived, left with half a face like that guy Jim he was in rehab with? Talking nasally even though there was no nose left? He would never get laid again with a face like that. Was it normal to think these things?

They stopped at a liquor store. Alcoholics scurried into the store shaking with blood shot eyes. "Got to use the bathroom. Grab what you want," Maceo said. America was a beer drinker. America believed in karma. America always wanted to be in control. She wasn't one to get too fucked up, but she did know how to have fun. She was ok when ankle deep in one of life's many storms, but when the dark cloud was painting shadows on the horizon--not knowing if it would be a hundred year flood or blown over by the wind, this was when her panic set in.

This whole suicide thing will pass, thought Maceo as he nodded at the mirror. He finished and walked out of the bathroom, he watched her figure through beer posters of half naked chicks. The top of her ear poked through her reddish hair lit by the sun. Maceo had always liked this. It reminded him of the Gelflings in the Dark Crystal, maybe it reminded him of childhood, or maybe it was the time they first met outside a bar on Abbot Kinney.

In the car America already had the whiskey cracked open, a cigarette smoldering in her hand, the window down, the day still young. He rubbed his face--an itch that only burrowed deeper. He looked at his eyes in the rear view—darkened from from all the rubbing. "I thought you only drank beer?" he asked.

"Let's get going. We have a big day," she said.

"You know Maceo, I've never felt like this before." She talked over the radio. "Even when me and mother were living hotel to hotel and I was pulling lit cigarettes from her fingers before she set another room on fire, somehow I always knew I'd be alright. Maybe I was young and naive, but I don't feel like that anymore," she said while looking at the mountains. "I have nobody. I am a disease. I have no one to love me."

Maceo pulled his head up and swerved back into the lane. His voice was slightly slurred, "I love you. Why is that not good enough?"

"Yeah you love anyone that has a vagina. You live halfway across the country. You can't hold me, kiss me, fuck me. You know how well I know my vibrator? I had to give it a name."

"Did you name it after me?"

"Hell no. I call him Prince."

"Because king was taken?" Maceo asked.

"No, because it's purple, like the rain."

He tried to look her in the eye, even though his own were colorless slits hanging from his face like a septuagenarian's breasts. "I wanted to apologize again for what I did. I feel horrible about it."

She pulled her hand from his and lit a cigarette. "Yeah, I bet it felt real horrible when your cock was in that little Russian slut." She took a drag and blew smoke in his direction. "How does it feel to fuck a communist?"

"Communisms' overrated," he said as he grabbed the bottle from her and tilted it back as if he were his prayer. "Somebody had to end the Cold War." It started to rain. The highway obsidian and broken windshield wipers made a sad attempt.

He had been clean for 784 days. All it took was America dumping him to pick up the needle again. First it was one time, like it always is. One time. The opiate washes out all the sad feelings through the fingertips, the toes, out with the soul. "You must love to get love in return," Maceo said quietly.

America laughed. "Are you reading the bible again?"

Maceo only read it when he was using. Hunting for an elusive one liner that would finally set him free of his addictions.

"No, self help books. Same thing I guess."

An eighteen wheeler shook the car. Maceo switched eyes.

"What the fuck is wrong with you?" America asked. "Look at you, you look like the god damned Hamburglar, are you using? I always said if you were using I'd dump you. My mom put me through enough shit with drugs."

"You already did dump my ass, and no, I'm not using. I just didn't get much sleep. I was so excited to see you." Maceo scratched his leg furiously.

She looked him up and down. "I trust you then."

"You do?"

"Of course I do. You might not be able to keep your dick in your pants but you've always kept your word. Like I'd ask a person I didn't trust to kill me."

"Does anybody know you are here?" Maceo asked.

"Nobody gives a fuck," she snapped.

He grabbed her hand and twisted her mood ring. She squirmed a bit but didn't pull away, lightly touching his fingers back, exploring cautiously like the first time. She pulled from the bottle. The oaky aroma of bourbon overtook the scent of her peach body lotion. America was warm with spirit, almost giddy. Maceo had never seen her use chemicals in this way. He wondered if she copped a drinking problem since they broke up.

The highway was plumb across the plains, the foothills ran along side the car always one step ahead holding them by a string looking back as a big brother does, pulling his younger sibling through a crowd. Big gray clouds hung in the sky. He pulled the contract from his pocket and handed it to her. She read over it.

"You're funny. You know I don't like Bob Dylan." She handed him the bottle as she read, sliding her hand into his, leaning a little closer, knees together. "Ok, sounds good. You got a pen?"

Maceo slammed the whiskey and wiped his mouth. "You really want to do it?"

"Of course. Why else would I come out here? Did you get the heroin?" she asked.

"Um, not yet."

She looked into his eyes, he couldn't look in hers. "You aren't very prepared then are you. Unless you did all of it already."

"I haven't done it in years, you know that."

She rested her head on his shoulder. Her forehead warm against his cheek. He hadn't felt human heat for months. He leaned into it.

"I can't believe you agreed to kill me. You jerk," she laughed. The promise of her laugh brought a tinge of clarity. He told him self he'd get clean once she went home. She turned her head and looked up at him.

The rain came down and she said, "I really do love you." He said the same thing not caring if she was drunk or not, the words still came from her mouth, their form crossed her mind at some point making them tangible.

She grabbed the contract and ripped it down the middle, throwing it out the window, pieces stuck to the side of the car.

Maceo took his eyes off the road to kiss her. Lips intertwined, the car started to careen in slow motion gently sideways until inertia became more than physics. "Maceo!" she screamed, nails dug into

into his arm. He over corrected. The car jumped the medium into oncoming traffic and started to roll. The radio fell silent. Everything slowed, he felt he could reach out and grab the bottle of whiskey, grab the odds and ends floating through the cab, hold America in her seat by throwing his weight on her, but in reality the world was spinning out of control. They were nothing but a satellite now, stuck by the laws of the universe. Out the window the mountains, headlights, the rain, the clouds, pavement, mountains, nothing, came and went, and came again. Once they came to a stop steam rose from the upside down carriage--the rain hitting hot metal. Maceo couldn't move, could only see black, could smell peaches through burnt rubber and whiskey. She was there. Somewhere. He felt no pain as the opiates worked even harder with each beat of his heart. Rain fell through the busted-out window and cleansed the blood from his face. "America?" He called out. Vehicles heading into oblivion, tires hissing through the storm was the only sound.

RD Armstrong
TWO DRINK MINIMUM

"COCK SUCKING SON OF A BITCH! You MISERABLE piece of goddamned cock sucking piece of shit!"

Across the room from me, Bob yelled for about the two hundredth time. It was eleven AM and he'd already had at least one beer. You see a lot of that in the trades. Lots of guys don't really get off the ground until they've had their morning tug. But most of those guys aren't ready to kill a piece of drywall because it could only behave like a piece of drywall, either.

Not so with Bob. He was ready to open up a big ol' can of whoopass on that piece of wallboard and was reaching for his trusty framing hammer.

"It needs a minor adjustment," he said, with just a hint of malice.

I thought the next words out of his mouth would be "It started it!" But was wrong when he screamed *cock sucking son of a bitch, miserable piece of goddamned cock sucking piece of shit!*

"Two hundred and one," I thought to myself.

"Am I doing this right?"

This, from my co-worker Helen, who was cute (in a sort of psychotically imbalanced and high maintenance way – in that way that bad girls get when they've been bad too long). Like Britney, the Pop icon...bad and slutty one minute and virginal and pissed off, the next. Like that.

Helen was scraping the wall a few feet to my left. She was working real hard; it was important to her that she do it right. I think she was trying to prove something to our boss...like the fact that she needed her job and he really could start trusting her again.

I watched her working. She was really tearing into her job. I looked at her form, the way she leaned into each stroke, the way her arms tightened up as she pulled back, her determined look as she focused on each new section...and yes, the way her tits bobbed. She had on the loosest undershirt I have ever seen. And every time she leaned over, there they were, on view for anyone interested. The guy across the way had made their acquaintance earlier and I'm sure, like me, he was wondering how long it would take before he made his move. I knew I had to make a sacrifice. I knew what I must do next.

"That looks fine, Helen, you're really giving it what for."

"Cock sucking son of a bitch! You miserable piece of godamned cock sucking piece of shit!"

"But I have to say that that shirt is giving me a problem."

"What? My shirt? What's wrong with my goddamned shirt?"

Oh boy.

"There's nothing wrong with your shirt except that it shows off your tits every time you bend over."

"What??? You're looking at my tits? Is that what you are saying? You..."

"Cock sucking son of a bitch!"

I had to turn away from her, for some reason this was suddenly very funny. It was like a Monty Python skit. I imagined myself in the Office of Bad Chemistry, being abused by John Clease. I hate to admit it but I was starting to enjoy this banter. Between the two of them it was quite a circus. Helen on one side firing the standard line of bullshit, laced with a healthy dose sexual innuendo and drug chatter; and Bob on the other devoting half the day to his new mantra, punctuating it with short protests of "aw, come on.." or "that's it baby, that's it..." It was a three ring circus. "Where the hell is *my* ring?" I wondered.

In construction work, it's not just the steelworkers who use crude language. In fact, these days you hear about people saying shit that they shouldn't all the time. It's a fact when you put men and women in the same room, someone's bound to get ideas or, worse, frisky. Helen and I traded smart-assed comments most of the day before. Yet, buried in all that, Helen also told me a lot about herself (I've learned to take notes when the cute –but dangerous-- chicks begin to drop innocent, little clues about why you should give them, at least, an extra car length). She was a real 'chatty Cathy', turns out. I soon realized that there was no way in hell that trying to get beyond her come-ons (and into her pants) was worth all the subsequent grief I would have to endure after we caught our breaths. I hated to give up the peep show, but it was just gonna make this...

"Cock sucking son of a bitch, miserable piece of godamned cock sucking piece of shit!"

...job that much harder to endure. And I had to endure it as long as I could because, like Helen, I needed the money. And unlike Helen, well more specifically, Helen's tits, I wasn't going to be able to sweet-talk the boss, if push came to shove. We both knew it; both knew she had the edge.

"So, you think it's my fault, you're a perve?"

Ah, the trump card!

"Hey, you don't care if we see your tits every time you bend over? Well, shit girl, take the damned thing off!" No sense in beating around the bush, I always say.

"Fuck you! There's nothing wrong with my shirt."

She was inspecting her shirt. She was right, when she stood up it was a nice, respectably loose shirt. But when she leaned over again, there they were, again. And I'd think "Hello girls!" This went on until Bob swore again and she stopped scraping and stood up very close to me, saying "I guess you're right, what do you think I should do about it? It's not like my tits are big enough to be a problem..."

"Your tits are just fine..." What was I saying? I sure didn't mind looking at them, but I knew that trouble was a'brewing because I was starting to think more about her tits than I was about the job at hand. So I had to either get her to cover up or just blow off the job and try and do her during lunch.

"How about putting on another shirt, weren't you wearing one earlier this morning?"

She looked at me and smiled and for a moment I was twenty years back in time in Hermosa Beach with my hands up Crazy Jane's shirt... And just like then, I watched as the shadows flickered across her eyes and *I knew* there was something way out of whack with her. In Crazy Jane's case, she was about to be labeled "certifiable." In Helen's case, I wasn't quite sure how close she was to the edge, but I knew that I didn't want to get sucked in (even "on" was losing its appeal). Except for the tits. They presented their case very well. Come to think of it, so did Crazy Jane's.

"Oh. Okay."

And like that she headed for the bathroom. Simple. Easy. A done deal. I went back to addressing the wall. I had to make it flat and there was a sizable indentation in it.

"Cock sucking son of a bitch, miserable piece of goddamned cock sucking piece of shit!"

I had to agree. Whoever built this apartment slash condo complex was either in a really big hurry or a complete moron. Come to think of it, they were probably both (I seem to recall there was some big scandal back in the early seventies when these things were built).

Helen came out of the bathroom. "I figured out what the problem was...it was my hair-do."

Hair-do? I looked over at her. She'd put it up in a bun of sorts. She came over to her spot on the wall and bent over to start scraping. "There, isn't that nicer?" She asked.

She was happy, her tits were happy. Who was I to upset the apple cart?

"Yeah, you're right, *that* was the problem. Yes sirree..."

"Cock sucking son of a bitch, miserable piece of goddamned cock sucking piece of shit!"

Geezus! I thought to myself, this guy is really starting to get to me. *But I should be able to get through this, I'm a fucking adult, right? I know what's what.*

Something came crashing across the room and bounced off the wall next to me. I turned around just in time to see a tape measure go skidding across the floor.

"Hey, you crazy motherfucker, knock that shit off!" I yelled over at him, looking at Helen who winced and bent over even farther.

"What'd you say?" Bob was turning towards me, slowly like he was going to say DRAW! next and whip out a hogleg the size of a canon. I'd managed to hit the 'whoopass' button on him and I could see it was gonna get ugly.

"I said, you crazy motherfucker, throwing your tools around like you were the only one in here. Get a fuckin' grip, man, it's embarrassing to listen to you. You're a man, act like one!"

Bob looked at me. Really, he gaped at me, mouth slightly ajar, as if he'd never heard this before and was now cut to the quick. I noticed he was missing a front tooth. *Why doesn't he have a lisp,* I wondered to myself?

"Did you call me...crazy? I'm not crazy, man, it ain't right to say that, man, it just ain't right. Cock sucking son of a bitch..." he muttered, his voice trailing off.

"Well, shit man, what am I supposed to think, when *you're* the one coming unglued, throwing your shit around? Is this what you call sane?"

Bob looked at me like he'd just been called to the Mother Superior's office for cussing. "It ain't right," he muttered under his breath, "you cock sucking son of a bitch, miserable piece of goddamned cock sucking piece of shit!" Then he turned around and began to use the hammer to punch holes in the wall. The wall put up a fight, but was no match for the hammer. Bob didn't care. He droned, "cock sucking son of a bitch, miserable piece of goddamned cock sucking piece of shit," muttering it low about every other hammer swing.

Whomp! Whomp!

"Cock sucking son of a bitch, miserable piece of goddamned cock sucking piece of shit!"

Whomp! Whomp!

"You cock sucking son of a bitch, miserable piece of goddamned cock sucking piece of shit!"

And so on.

It was like a cross between Queen's "We Will Rock You" and Pink Floyd's "Money" (just the opening). I found myself smiling. The humor was fleeting. As the mantra continued, old Bob began to get more excited. Pretty soon the whomping was replaced with a crashing sound as Bob threw the hammer down, shattering a tile at his feet. He spun around to face the room and began to say, very, very slowly, like James Cagney might say in an old movie, you know, right before he pumps a shot or two into George Raft:

"YOU...DIRTY...MOTHERFUCKING...COCK   SUCKING... SON OF A...BITCH!"

This was followed by a slow burn. I was surprised that Bob could do a slow-burn since he was such a hot-head...but there it was. You could almost imagine the steam coming out of his ears as he continued:

"MISERABLE...PIECE   OF...GODAMNED...   COCK SUCKING... PIECE... OF... SHIT!"

This last part, was said with such vehemence, I half expected blood to shoot out of his eyes, or things to start exploding around me, like in a bad Stephen King movie.

"Bob, honey? Can I do something to help?" It was Helen. It was a girlish voice. I looked at her. Her tits were not girlish, but her current personality was. It was unsettling. Another 'red flag.' So all that banter about her fucked up marriage was true. I was pretty sure that her childhood wasn't that uneventful either. She had the whole slut/ saint/wounded deer thing wired. It had served her well over the years. She was 'daddy's girl' and working it quite well. I had already started calling her 'Princess.'

Like me, Bob was looking at her tits, mesmerized really. "You can have 'em," I thought and went back to work. I heard him say to her, over my shoulder, "Well, yeah, Helen, there is this one thing you can do for me..."

Here it comes...

"...you could come over here and scrape this wall for me and..." It trailed off. I heard her move over there. They started to talk, or so I thought, but it was just their slowly escalating mantras of "cock sucking son of a bitch, miserable piece of goddamned cock sucking piece of shit" and "there's nothing wrong with my shirt."

I was making some progress on the wall. It was looking like it might work out okay. Bob had settled down. I guess Helen's breasts had soothed the savage beast (or however that saying goes). She came back over to 'our' wall and began to scrape. It was good to see her and her friends again. The world was right at last. Even the radio, which had been blaring out 'speed-metal' (the industry standard, when it comes to demolition) most of the morning, was playing some sentimental rock ballad. I sighed. It was good to be here, now.

Suddenly my reverie was broken by Bob's overly dramatic rendition of the chorus. He was really getting into it. Of course, he couldn't sing for shit. In fact, there wasn't a bucket made that was big enough for him to carry this tune in!"
"Well at least he's not yelling." I thought.

Ah, innocence.

"Cock sucking son of a bitch, miserable piece of goddamned cock sucking piece of shit!"

I'd had it. Screw the cautious-I'm-not-gonna-come-down-to-his-level approach.

"Bob? Why don't you shut the fuck up?"

"Cock sucking son of a...what'dya just say?" Bob turned slowly. He had this vein on his forehead that looked like it was two beats away from exploding. "What did you say?" He asked again.

"Oh shit, now you've done it." Helen said cringing lower to the floor. She was probably right. But even a mature adult like me could only take so much.

Bob was back to muttering under his breath, "that just ain't right, telling me to shut the fuck up...cock sucking, son of a..."

"Bob? You got another beer? You better take a break right now."

I watched him warily, while he moved across the room and out onto the balcony, where his beer stash was. He lit a cigarette and opened a beer. I waited. I knew that the shit was drifting towards the fan, that soon he'd be ready to defend his 'honor'. Bob finished his smoke and slammed the remains of the beer. He turned to face me.

I looked at my watch. It was almost one o'clock, just in time for the matinee.

"All right, motherfucker, let's git to it."

Michael D. Meloan
MAMAN

MAMAN LIKES TO PAINT in the living room while drinking big tumblers of Tab and Vodka and listening to Josh White records. She paints nudes with big bushy black pubic hair. It's embarrassing when my friends come over, but she doesn't care; she paints and paints and paints.

Maman took art classes, but she said they were holding her back and forcing her into an unnatural style. As she steps back from her canvass, she takes a sip from a straw and squints. She is working on a painting of a woman with big sagging tits and short dark hair. The woman has a defiant expression and her head is tilted slightly sideways, so she's looking at you from the corner of her slitty eyes. She's holding two bright yellow grapefruit. There are colors flying all over the place.

Staley and Falk ring the doorbell on Friday night. They are standing there with a huge load of music equipment. My father has been out of town all week on a business trip, and won't be back for another few days. So Maman said that we could set up the amp and play electric guitars in the rumpus room while she paints. My father doesn't approve of the arts. He says art is an expression of the neurotic impulse.

Staley and Falk haul the Fender Super Reverb inside the door and across the living room. Then they plug in the Teisco Del Rey guitar, the St. George bass, and a skinny silver Radio Shack mic on a tall chrome stand. Staley kicks in the fuzz boxes and starts playing rhythmic barred chords, while Falk makes throbbing noises with the bass. I chant words into the mic, making them up as I go. Maman is grooving with it, nodding her head up and down; then she takes another big sip of her drink. When she stops to go to the bathroom, I walk around behind

95

the wooden bar and grab a bottle of Early Times bourbon. I pour half of my Coke down the stainless steel drain, and fill the rest of the can up with bourbon. By the time Maman comes back from the bathroom, the bottle is back underneath the bar.

As we play, I take drinks. It tastes like shit, but I drink it anyway. I've had booze before, but I've never been really drunk. I feel like I'm on my way. The telephone rings, and she walks out of the room. I open another Coke, pour half out again, and fill it up with whisky. It's starting to taste better. I'm swaying, holding on to the microphone with my eyes closed, and coming up with some good shit.

"You should always get drunk," says Staley. "You're better this way."

Maman walks back into the room. "That was your father. He wanted to know what all the noise was about."

"Tell him you're having a party," I say as I start laughing. I can't help myself. I take another drink of whisky Coke. "Tell him the Black Panthers dropped by for cocktails."

She laughs, "He doesn't understand that kind of humor. There would just be silence on the other end of the line." Then she peers at me, "Have you been drinking? You seem high."

"I had a couple of whisky Cokes," I say.

"If your father knew I was letting you drink, he'd just shit," she says. "But what the hell. I'd rather you got drunk at home."

She walks across the room and goes behind the wet bar. Then she pulls out a bottle of Bourbon, a bottle of Vodka, and a bottle of Tom Collins mixer. She walks to the kitchen with an ice bucket and comes back with it filled, on a tray, with some hi-ball glasses. Ice cubes fly from her chrome tongs and race around the bottoms of the glasses. Staley and Falk set their instruments down and come over to sit on the tall black Naugahyde bar stools. Maman is wearing a scoop neck lemon yellow blouse with tight black stretch pants, and she's barefoot. At one point, I see Falk's eyes drop down and look at her breasts. She pours some of the mix into each of the four glasses, then measures out healthy shots of Kamchatka vodka and dumps it into each of the glasses. Then she slices some limes in two and squeezes juice into the drinks. She raises her glass and looks at each of us.

"Old pond, frog jumps in—plop," she says laughing and clinking her glass against each of ours. Staley starts laughing, and takes a big drink.

"Your mother is a trip," says Falk.

We all drink, and it goes down easy now. Maman starts making more cocktails. She lights up a cigarette.

"I'm not allowed to smoke when the old man is at home. He has asthma, you know," she says to Staley and Falk.

We have one more cocktail, and I'm feeling like I want to jam some more. We all light up cigarettes. Staley and Falk plug back in and start playing soft but fast. Maman comes up to the microphone, and begins singing. It's kind of jazzy, and as she laughs the reverb echoes. She is chanting as she strokes the microphone with her slender white fingers.

"I was a beatnik baby on the lower east side," she talk-sings. "My roommate was a blond bombshell who had to run and hide. She ended up a concubine -- one of Josh White's women. He only dated white, very white, very pretty white women. Only pretty-pretty white women. My other roommate was Mae Brown - a bull dike who liked to sleep around. She wore a greasy jelly roll. She only dated pretty white women. Only pretty-pretty white women. I smoked a little reefer now and then. She wanted to make love to me. Now and then. Making love … with pretty white women."

"Your mother's better than you are!" says Falk.

"Yeah, I think he's right. She is better," Staley says to me, smoking his cigarette.

I go back to the bar and pour two fingers of Early Times into my glass, and some Coke. Then I drink it down. Maman is back over at her canvas. She has switched back to Tab and vodka, and is busy studying her painting. Staley and Falk are sitting on the couch in the living room, drinking their drinks and watching her. The amplifier is buzzing alone in the rumpus room. I walk up to her, and I feel something coming on, like a jolt of powerful mania.

"In the future, you'll just plug-in your mind and let it spew. A faucet on the side of your head, turn it all the way on and let the colors and shapes gush out onto the floor. Stir it around with a broom and there you go. And go, and go. No practice required, no paint, no brushes, no canvases. No nothing! And no excuses -- just you and your naked brain. Oop-bipp-bipp, Oop-bipp-bipp, YEAH! Do you hear me!" I scream. "My mind has wings. Do you believe me YEAH!!!" I scream at the top of my lungs. She turns nonchalantly to me, taking a puff from her cigarette.

"If you say so," she says.

"I say so! In fact, let me prove it to you! Let me paint. I'll show you how to really paint. How to tap right into your mind." I try to grab her paint brush, but she wrestles it out of my hand.

"You're out of control! No more liquor!" she says.

"I don't need more liquor. I've got everything I need. My nervous system is about to leave this star cluster. I'm like a German nuclear engine. I want to show you something!" Staley and Falk are just sitting there smoking and watching. I walk across the room, and pick up the cheap acoustic guitar that I bought down in Tijuana. I strum the same chord over and over and chant, "Everybody's talkin' 'bout the seventh son, in the whole damn world there is only one. I'm the one. Everybody's talkin' bout the seventh son, in the whole damn world there is only one. I'm the one. No more musical instruments!" I scream.

Then I grab the guitar by its neck, raise it high over my head and smash it on the brick steps that lead from the rumpus room to the living room. I smash it three times before the sound box comes loose and is shattered into splinters.

"No! Stop!" Maman is screaming as she comes running toward me. Staley and Falk are sitting there smiling. I walk over to the bar to get another drink. As I am pouring the whisky into the glass, she grabs the bottle and tries to wrestle it out of my hand. I pick up the hi-ball glass and gulp down the little bit of whisky that ended up in the bottom. Then I open the sliding glass door and run out to the back yard. I wind up and hurl the glass over the top of the house.

"My God!" she screams, "are you out of your mind?"

"It's all your fault. You wanted to compete with me!"

"You remind me of my drunken father!" she screams.

"Let's get out of here," I say to Staley and Falk.

"Where do you want to go, man?" asks Staley.

"Anywhere, let's just cruise. Maybe we should go to Hollywood and pick up some chicks."

"That might be cool," Staley says. Staley has a license, and he has his own car.

"Nobody's going anywhere," says Maman. "Not after I provided the booze. Give me your car keys!" She reaches into Staley's pocket, and tries to get his keys.

"Now listen, pretty Momma. You just stepped way out of bounds," he says. He jerks her hand out of his pocket and shoves her hard. She spins all the way around and loses her balance, then falls backward onto her butt. As she sits in the middle of the living room floor, looking slightly dazed, Staley and Falk start laughing and I see red. Before there is thought, my fist connects with Staley's face and a shock wave goes through my arm. There's a crunching sound, and he goes down holding his nose. I feel disconnected, like I'm watching a movie.

"You fucker! Why'd you do that? The bitch was out of control."

"Nobody pushes her down like that! Understand? Nobody!" I scream.

Staley struggles up still holding his nose. Blood is streaming down his arms, and his shirt is stained red. I can smell the blood. He moves to the front door, turns and looks at me with hate, then slams it hard. Falk walks slowly across the living room shaking his head, then follows Staley out the door. Maman is still on her butt in the middle of the living room carpet. I walk over and offer her my hand. As I am pulling her up, she looks into my eyes; then starts laughing.

"I haven't seen that kind of action since I lived in New York. You remind me of my old boyfriend Ivan. He was a Trotskyite, and a mad painter. If someone looked at me the wrong way, he beat them up. It was very exciting." She lights a cigarette and walks over to the wet bar. As she grabs an ice cube with her chrome tongs, she turns to look at me again, with the cigarette dangling from her lips and her eyes squinting from the smoke. It's the same defiant look as the woman in her painting.

"It's good to have a man around the house," she says after a long pause. Then she puts her cigarette down in the ashtray, parts her lips slightly, and walks slowly toward me.

John Macker
NOT TOO FAR FROM THE MAVERICK BAR

> *"How much does a man live, after all?*
> *Does he live a thousand days or one only?*
> *For a week, or for several centuries?*
> *How long does a man spend dying?*
> *What does it mean to say for ever?"*
>
> *—Neruda*

I'M JUST A COUPLE OF MILES from the border under a searing sun. I'm surrounded by organ pipe and thin-limbed ocotillo blooming. To my left are the Ajo Hills. Behind me are the Puerto Blanco mountains. I've driven down here to bury my dog, Bill. I am a journalist and just south of here, it's open season on us. I am also a poet. I've written screenplays that have no life beyond the page. I've worked as a boxer and summons server. Been married three times. I'm an alcoholic. The last book I read (I think) was House of Spirits.

This desert is my sin and my penance.

This is where my soul comes to pray for rain.

Back home in New Mexico, I packed my dog in dry ice in a canvas bag and put him in the back of my Ford Ranger. I have slung the canvas bag full of Bill and a camp shovel over my shoulder and started walking. This country is pockmarked with old silver mines and dried snake rattles. One mine, the Victoria, a half mile or so ahead, was abandoned in the 1920's. Most of its holes are boarded up. Except for the graffiti and vandalism, the desert is taking it back. There is a roofless stone shack with wooden window frames. High noon in this stupefacient heat and I can see a chorus line of imaginary hoodoos, dust devils, shadows no longer of use and baked into the earth like desiccated angels and the footprints I made when I came here as a child with my mother, in a battered station wagon, her bruised marriage to my stepfather in ruins. I remember we camped out here for days. The past has locked onto me from high above, like a predator drone.

Look through the glare, the dust, the border endgame, and you can get to who you once were. Find yourself and everyone you once loved in a mosaic of brittle bones bleached on the desert pavement. No fucking scorpions crawling across the mirrors on your hobnail boots out here middle of the day. No landforms lifted from some Georgia O'Keeffe painting. My mother's ferocious heart returned here every time it rained. I can see a lone hummingbird hover at a deep red ocotillo blossom. The only sound for miles, that insatiable buzz. There's a clear blue sky and the heat has a peculiar, callous weight to it. I set my bag down. I don't have far to go. : "And that is how/all the nights go over/ the earth. Hell, I can reach Gallup, New Mexico and the Maverick Bar in just a few hours; the last place I did any meaningful drinking. In those days, apropos my whoring nature, I'd drink with anyone.

Charles Bukowski is at the bar nursing a Pacifico and I want to tell him how much I've admired his poem, On The Fire Suicides of the Buddhists… but there isn't much time. The sun has reached its zenith and all is quiet except for a dull blessing of a breeze wafting up from Mexico. Off in the distance I can see a couple of border trekkers, gallon plastic jugs of water in their hands; they're moving deliberately in and out of arroyos as if bobbing on waves, eyes focused away from the cauterizing sun. Absolutely, the only thing this heat is good for is destroying aberrant tissue. They don't dare look back. The heat would immobilize anything not destined for eternity.

I figure I owe Bill this much. I'm sweating more with each shovelful. He followed our bitch German Shepard home one day, I fed him once and he never left. He had the run of the joint. He was a small dog but he fought a wolf hybrid twice his size to a bloody stand-off. One summer night, after we held him down and pulled the porcupine quills from his face, all that was left was bumpy swollen gore. He was unequivocally my dude dog. I think I named him after the pimply faced gunslinger who wouldn't be pardoned, not even 130 years after his death.

It is a grave and it is shallow, I finish it off with a pile of rocks to keep the coyotes from him. My eyes are seeing cinders and white flashes of stinging sweat. It's as if the desert is testifying on the silence deep within it, above it, this place where the borderless soul knows nobody is pitied or redeemed or reclaimed by prayer. I toss the camp shovel into the bag.

There is a vague, smoky essence to the breeze, now. A rosaceous full moon rises low over the desert like the blood of Christ.

It is a temptation to want to go there, with them, to where they were and are, once and for all, to follow their tracks deep into the earth that hold the stones in place, with the hard sun glowering down on them while the rest of the world merrily conspires in the madness. But the silence, this sizzling epic of silence, turns me for home.

(Previously published in Tree Killer Ink #10 - *Alberta, Canada)*

Marc Olmsted
GOOD SIGN

BETH CUT HAIR out of her Mission St. apartment. She was a big girl, tattooed, jet black hair and red lipstick in Goth nod, and she was married to Gomez, a butcher from Mexico, who for some reason didn't have a green card, probably because they never could make any deadline or appointment that would give it to him.

Problem was, Gomez was abusive. For 9 years he'd punched her for just about anything he could think of. The bruises rarely if ever showed. None of Beth's friends or hairstyle clients knew anything about it.

Gomez got a role in a local indie movie and this made him think he was a star. He didn't want Beth to go the local premiere but she thought he was kidding. Gomez really did want to go alone (she later thought because he didn't want to share the spotlight, but I suspect he was looking for some new trim, no pun intended).

Well, she went anyway and when they came home and walked in the door he turned and punched her twice in the eye and took this campy Jesus statue they had and broke it on her body. He hit her so hard in the eye she thought she'd gone blind. She did, for a bit. She called the police as she'd done before.

When she went downstairs from the 3rd floor to let them in the gate, there was something about their vibe that made her pause. They didn't like that. There were way more cops than she ever anticipated, at least 2 squad cars with flashing lights and some more cops on foot. She was right about their vibe. When she opened the gate, they cuffed her and led her away. She was barefoot and wasn't wearing a bra under her t-shirt. She wasn't ready to go out into the night. She didn't even get to lock her apartment door. She'd also had too much to drink.

Gomez came back while they were taking Beth away and walked right into them. He had decided to use the "What's this, officer?" approach and act like nothing had happened. They took him away too.

Beth actually knew some of these cops, because they were local. That didn't do any good now. She was chained to a wall for 10 hours without water. It was very cold. They gave her some old dirty socks for her feet. No blanket, though. Beth said the female cops were the worst.

Eventually they put her in with the recently captured crack whores. One was a white girl with dreads, but claimed to be a skinhead affiliate. Beth asked about the dreads, since the white girl, a runaway who voraciously read, was spouting all sorts of Neo-Nazi rhetoric and Beth wondered why she'd picked the dreadlocks if she hated blacks so much. The reason was utilitarian. Still, the neo-Nazi girl knew that some of the black women, trustees who'd been in a while and were allowed to roam relatively free in exchange for cleaning the place, would find the shit she'd pinched off in the shower. They did, and they thought it was Beth at first. Beth's bad day looked like it was about to get worse, but fortunately they figured out that Neo-Nazi girl did it. No witness as to what happened to her sorry Nazi ass.

Monday finally rolled around, and after being seen in cuffs by some of her own hairstyle clients who worked the local precinct, they let her go now two days later and all charges were dropped. Not before the girl cop moved her for processing, though, putting the cuffs on Beth's wrists so tight that her hands turned blue.

Beth went home on the morning bus. She had a little orange band on her wrist from jail. It meant a free bus ride. Whoo-whoo! They also gave these oversized flip flops for her bare feet. It was a long walk to the bus stop. She hung her head on the bus and vibed "Please don't look at me."

When she got home, the apartment door was still open. She discovered that clients had come for their appointments and found this weirdness. They never returned, despite her explanations. Some people.

Gomez was sent to Arizona for deportation to Mexico. He was there for 2 months before he agreed to voluntarily go back across the border. Otherwise, he might very well still be there.

It was of course a very good thing for Beth, who once away from him without any possibility of getting him back in the country, experienced enormous relief, though she hated to be alone. She fixed that pretty quick, but at least the new guy, also Latin, didn't hit.

The local cops still said hello like nothing had happened.

She got a banishing candle from the local botanica. When she burnt it, she saw a black shape like a medium sized dog with a blanket over it scoot out of the closet and go out the door. Good sign.

ESSAYS

BUKOWSKI

Claudio Parentela

Michael Meloan
A BUK REMEMBRANCE

WHEN I WAS SIXTEEN, my friends and I cruised Sunset Strip and brought back the LA Free Press, which ran Bukowski's column "Notes of a Dirty Old Man." We sat inside a backyard plywood shed that one of the neighborhood fathers had built to keep us out of trouble. As we smoked Tareytons and drank Colt 45, we read the column out loud. It was an explosion of hookers, philosophers, madmen and racetrack junkies. My early education.

Fifteen years later, my girlfriend Jan was working at the Dew Drop Inn, a health food restaurant in South Redondo. One day she mentioned that the owner, Linda Lee Beighle, was dating a poet named Charles Bukowski. There he was again.

A few months later, I visited the Dew Drop for lunch. Bukowski unexpectedly walked in, spitting venom because his Mac had somehow deleted a couple of new poems. Linda mentioned that I was a software guy.

"Are you any good?" he asked.

My father taught me always to say yes. A few hours later, the poems were back, and we sat drinking red wine while he asked me questions about how computers might be used to predict winners at the racetrack.

In the fall of that year, Bukowski invited me over for the evening. Just the two of us and his beloved plastic goose with a light bulb inside. He uncorked the first bottle of red.

"You seem a little nervous, kid," he said, pouring.

I took a big drink. I was nervous. But after a few glasses, the night took off. We were laughing and drinking until 3 a.m. With a stubby Indian Beedi dangling from his lips, he flicked his butane lighter a few times. A flame suddenly shot up like a hissing blowtorch.

His left eyebrow sizzled and crackled as he jerked his head back and went, "Arrrrgh!"

Later, he told me that I danced with the goose on my head and recited a long raving monologue about sex and death and science. I don't remember any of it, but he always did.

Hank's reputation for wildness was the real thing. At one of his Fourth of July bashes, he got an early start drinking, and decided the party was a bore.

He stormed around the living room demanding, "Where's your drink?!"

My brother Steve raised his glass and said, "This is my drink- Calistoga water!" A woman talking with him was sipping lemonade.

Clenching a Beedi, Bukowski sneered, "Get out! I want everybody out!"

At first we thought he was kidding, then he roamed the rooms screaming, "Get out! Get out! I might die tomorrow, and I don't want to spend my last night on earth with this bunch. Get the fuck out of my house! I want everybody OUT!"

As people wandered down the long driveway toward the street, two tall blond guys were hovering near the mailbox at the curb.

In heavy German accents, they asked, "This is the home of Bukowski, yes?"

"Yes," I said.

"What is going on?"

"He's on a rampage because we weren't drinking enough," I replied.

"This is very cool," the guy said grinning. "Very Bukowski."

* * *

But nights like that were rare. On any random evening, Hank was hard at work. One of his most important attributes was his discipline. He wrote every day – sick, exhausted, hung over – it didn't matter. He told me that he was like a spider building a web, it was in his DNA to pound the typer.

In a one-on-one encounter, Hank demanded your complete attention, even when he was drunk. Sitting on the couch in the living room, he would take a drink, then a drag, and his eye would cut over at you. Scrutinize you. There was no place to hide.

He was complex. Outrageous and sensitive. Loyal to his friends. When I was breaking up with Jan, he called to see how I was doing. He knew I was depressed and suggested that I come over for a drink. When I got there, Linda poured three glasses of good Cabernet. We talked for a while, and I told Hank that a literary agent had contacted me after I had some fiction published in WIRED magazine. I asked him what he thought about agents.

He paused, took a long drag, and said: "Listen kid...the whole thing comes down to this: If you want to write, you're going to write, and you'd better write it your way. If you're after money or fame or groupies, that's something else. Then you'll do it their way...and they will smash you down into a flattened turd." He took a big drink, then cut his eye over at me smiling and said, "Ring the bells of the city...the old man has spoken."

Alexandre Thiltges
"BUKOWSKI AND THE ROMANTIC INFLUENCE: WRITING AS A MEANS OF TRANSGRESSION"

WORDSWORTH WROTE in the preface of Lyrical Ballads: "Is there then, it will be asked, no essential difference between the language of prose and metrical composition? I answer that there neither is nor can be any essential difference." This declaration is strikingly reminiscent of Bukowski's vision of poetry as well as prose. Indeed, the syntax and style of Bukowski's poetical work are similar to the ones he uses in his prose, which constitutes the identity and originality of the Bukowskian poetics. Wordsworth wrote that "The principal object then which I proposed to myself in these Poems was to make the incidents of common life interesting [...]" The themes developed in Bukowski's writing are most of the time slices of life. The narrative style of his poetry is therefore intrinsic to the stylistic technique and identity of the text, which constitutes the main legacy Bukowski brought to contemporary American poetry. Wordsworth's attitude, as well as Bukowski's, underlines the fact that poetry should be removed from its pedestal: "Of the same substance, their affections are kindred and almost identical, not necessarily differing even in degree." He continues with the same tone: "But Poets do not write for Poets alone, but for men. [...] The Poet must descend from this supposed height." The role of the poet is on the contrary to understand mankind, from the "lower" to the "higher" social class, in order to re-transcript its language and emotions: "The language of such poetry as I am recommending is, as far as possible, a selection of the language really spoken by men." If Wordsworth knew how to express his conception about what poetry should be, his narrative technique can still be considered "elitist" and somehow "pedantic." Certain readers will indeed argue that one had to wait for a poet such as Bukowski to put this theory into practice. Wordsworth could not prevent from using figures of speech that were still abusively "poetic," and which may nowadays appear as extremely "artificial," contradicting his purpose. Bukowski gets rid of such language and focuses on the vernacular, spoken American English of his period of time. Then should be raised the question of the audience: whom is the poet writing for? If Wordsworth advocates the use of a language "really spoken by man," trying to make the "common life" events appear interesting, he still addresses his poems to a very restrained and selected public, which could certainly not be qualified as "common." Bukowski, on the other hand, who addresses his poetry to the "common man," is the first American poet to be read by the working class. Wordsworth's vision of what poetry should be is nevertheless very similar to Bukowski's. Just like Wordsworth, Bukowski often incorporates dialogue into his poetry, gives it a narrative function and includes subjects of everyday life.

Wordsworth's revolutionary conception of poetry has also obviously influenced American writers such as Whitman, who believed that writing should be democratized, used a familiar and vernacular language and wrote about taboo and sexual subjects while emphasizing the importance of personal experience. Writing becomes therefore an introspective method allowing the reader to discover his profound self, a predominating theme in Bukowski's poetry and fiction.

Whitman's work offers many similarities with Bukowski's. Despite his optimistic beliefs in the American democracy, Whitman wrote in his essay entitled "Democratic Vistas," echoing Thoreau's Civil Disobedience:

The depravity of the business classes of our country is not less than has been supposed, but infinitely greater. The official services of America, national, state, and municipal, in all their branches and departments, except the judiciary, are saturated in corruption, bribery, falsehood, mal-administration; and the judiciary is tainted. The great cities reek with respectable as much as non-respectable robbery and scoundrelism....I say that our New World democracy....is, so far, an almost complete failure.

This doubt concerning the honesty of men in power and this conviction that the governmental institutions are inhumane, corrupted machines, is also one of the messages that can be found in Bukowski's work. In his first two novels, whose central themes concern the working world, the individual is depicted as totally powerless against the monstrosity of the system. The violence of the Bukowskian stylistic technique corresponds therefore to the feelings of revolt animating the alienated characters found in the text.

Bukowski has often been perceived as an anti-American writer, even though he belongs to a school of thinking that is absolutely American, as Jules Smith noted:

He thereby joins a lengthy list of American writers who conceived themselves as rugged individualists, anti-aesthete aesthetes, and Advertisers for the Self: Thoreau, Melville, Twain, Whitman, Jack London, Jeffers, Hemingway, Miller, Mailer, most of the Beats, Ken Kesey and many others. Bukowski emerged in a culture that stresses individual freedoms and distrusts collectivity.

Rebellion against the institution that maintains the individual in an alienated position is by any means a value deeply rooted in the

American culture. America was founded on a precept of religious, political and economic "freedom." It is therefore not surprising that this abstract and ambiguous concept appears with such strength in its literature. Whitman and Bukowski's poetry, as we will see, can be characterized by a thematic and stylistic freedom. This notion of liberty is closely linked, in this young America, to the concept of individualism on which the "American spirit" was founded. The use of the signifier "individualism" is quite recent, since it only started to spread in the mid 18th century, exactly at the same period of time when the first stones of the American mythology where carved. Jean-Pierre Fichou writes in La Civilisation américaine that individualism "signifies in the United States 'the affirmation of the rights of the individual and of the group against the organism' and, by extension, 'protection of the little cultural entities against the big ones'" . The mythological figures of the cowboy, the pioneer and the self-made-man are all created around the first person singular. This "I" refers to the individual cut from the group, "I" for whom this America represents the land of freedom of thought and expression. Chinaski, who rebels against the institutions encroaching upon his individual freedom, uses his writing as a means of expression allowing him to affirm himself as an individual. Individualism, in Bukowski's novels, is marked by the narrative technique itself, since the narrator writes exclusively in the first person singular. The Bukowskian model thus becomes an introspective and narcissistic one, based on the research and affirmation of the self. Anika Lemaire writes that the grammatical category 'I' is the clue of individuality, because it cannot be conceived without the 'you', without the 'he' nor without the auditor against who it is opposed.

As E. Benveniste notes in General Linguistics Problems: it is in and by language that man constitutes himself as a subject because only language founds in reality the concept of Self: 'is Self which says Self.'

Bukowski's œuvre is inscribed in a purely American tradition, responding to the one of Walt Whitman, and especially to "Song of Myself," whose first verse starts with "I celebrate myself." The poem entitled "Inscripts" echoes the previous one: "One's-self I sing, One's-self I sing, a single separate person." Concerning the poet, Whitman writes: "he is individual... he is complete in himself... the others are as good as he, only he sees it and they do not." The access to the Lacanian Symbolic order, to language, then to writing itself, is therefore responsible for the process of individualization. The rejection of the Other, the passage to the stage of the lion in the Nietzschean metamorphosis , allows the writer to later separate himself from the

Other and to become a total and complete individual.

Whitman and Bukowski are both the poets of the self, of urbanity, of modernity, and despite certain ideological divergences (for instance, Whitman's enthusiasm regarding the United States and his belief in democracy), they both elaborate their work around a similar theme. Whitman's style also shares many similarities with Bukowski's. Whitman's verses, as well as Bukowski's, do not rhyme nor do they respect traditional metric, rhythmic or versification rules. They have their proper rhythm, which critique first perceived as an unforgivable affront to Poetry. Whitman's style is also very sober, bare, which is translated into a conception of writing corresponding to a philosophy of life: "The art of art, the glory of expression and the sunshine of the light of letters is simplicity. Nothing is better than simplicity..." Bukowski makes the same point: "An intellectual is a man who says a simple thing in a difficult way; an artist is a man who says a difficult thing in a simple way." Echoing Wordsworth, Whitman praises what he calls in Leaves of Grass "the common people" . The narrator of Leaves of Grass claims indeed to represent the oppressed and the outcast, which corresponds again to a Bukowskian theme:

Through me many long dumb voices
Voices of the interminable generations of slaves,
Voices of Prostitutes and of deformed persons,
Voices of the diseased and the despairing, and of thieves and dwarfs,
[...] Of the trivial and flat and foolish and despised, [...]

"Slaves," "prostitutes," "despairing," "thieves," all of the outsiders and outcasts of this marvelous Promised Land, constitute also the archetypal characters filling the Bukowskian narrative space. Indeed, the function of Bukowski and Whitman's work is to express what has been censored and to transgress the forbidden:

Through me forbidden voices,
Voices of sexes and lusts... voices veiled, and I remove the veil,
Voices indecent by me clarified and transfigured.
I do not press my finger across my mouth,
I keep as delicate around the bowels as around the head and heart,
Copulation is no more rank to me than death is.

Whitman's writing, just like Bukowski's, is therefore symptomatic of the Lacanian return of the Real. Bukowski and Whitman do not hesitate describing man in its most animal and carnal way: "I believe in the flesh and appetites," writes Whitman, who wants to share through his work his vision of humanity as it is, and not as it has been fantasized. It thus became of higher importance for him to develop certain themes that were condemned by the moral of his time, such as sexuality, maternity, carnal desires, homosexuality and so forth. Just like Nietzsche, Gide, then Bukowski, Walt Whitman thought that the poet had to transmit a certain "Truth" and should consequently not hesitate to endorse the role of the immoralist: "The greatest poet does not moralize or make applications of morals... He knows the soul." It is not surprising that he became the target of the critique, which qualified Leaves of Grass of "Poetry of barbarism," "noxious weeds," "spasmodic idiocy," and even of "a mass of stupid filth." Like Bukowski, Whitman was often considered a "dirty old man," was poorly understood at the beginning of his career, and was only recognized after his death. Let's compare a few biographical facts about these two writers:

	Whitman	Bukowski
Year of birth	1819	1920
Year of death	1892	1994
Year of the beginning of fame	1871	1971
and age	52	51

Almost a century apart, these two "rebel-writers" have known a very similar career: they both encountered success at an older age (in their fifties), before dying relatively famous twenty years later. Isn't the function of the poet to denounce lies, to transgress taboos, and to make reappear the Id hidden in society, contained for too long, to the surface of the collective consciousness? The violence of Whitman's œuvre made his contemporary fellows feel so uncomfortable that one had to wait for many decades before he became recognized as a genius, and later, as the greatest American writer of all time.

Williams Carlos Williams' vision of poetry is also in a certain way very close to Bukowski's. William's famous declaration, "A free verse for a free country," linking the signifier to the signified, resonates in Bukowski's poetic oeuvre. The author uses a vernacular American language and chooses a style (signifiers) that corresponds to the themes he is dealing with (signifieds), concerning the working class, bars, the racing track... Bukowski's verses have themselves a free rhythm: they do not rhyme, can be extended on the whole line or be constituted of a short syntagm and sometimes a single syllable. Bukowski's poems cut themselves from a certain conservative tradition whose goal it is to preserve poetry as a "superior" genre connected to the "sacred." This modern conception of writing is close to the one of the Formalists, who perceived language as a tool allowing the deviation of a norm. This deviation appears in Bukowski's poetics through certain unexpected elements, such as a return to the line, which accentuates a syncopation of the syntax, the unexpected use of capital letters, italics or slang terms. According to Terry Eagleton, literature is constituted of "a kind of linguistic violence: literature is a 'special' kind of language in contrast to the 'ordinary' language we commonly use." Roman Jakobson writes that literature is a type of writing representing "an organized violence committed on ordinary speech." The function of literature would therefore be to transform and intensify the language of "everyday life."

The concepts of deviation and transgression are essential in Bukowski's writing, and are once again a reminder of the legacy of Romanticism in his work. The writer explains in the preface of one of his poetry collections: "It appears that certain people think that poetry should be a certain way. For these, there will be nothing but trouble years. More and more people will come along to break their concepts. It's hard, I know, like having somebody fuck your wife while you are at work, but life, as they say, goes on." The thematic of writing as a means of transgression appears clearly here in a stylistic way through the choice of the final metaphor as well as through the use of the slang terminology. We need to remember what Barthes had to say about the text as a means of transgression: "The text is (should be) this insolent and casual person who is to show his behind to the Political Father." Writing would therefore become a tool allowing the expression of revolt, an expression which can only be realized with style. Bukowski deliberately attacked through his writing the "academic" values and what could be generally called the "Canons of Literature." He concluded his career with the corrosive exergue: "dedicated to bad writing," which was a sardonic answer and a slap in the face to a literary critique that took too long before recognizing his talent. Under an appearance of nonchalance, the tone of this exergue should be interpreted as a revenge of the artist against the institutions. Neeli Cherkovski wrote in a book about the influence of Whitman on the most famous American poets: "Since Whitman, the 'writer as rebel' has become a tradition. Charles Bukowski is the most adamant among them in turning his back to academia. 'Whores, hospitals, and jails, these are the universities of life from which I hold several degrees,' he once wrote." Following Whitman's tradition, Bukowski's writing is the writing of rebellion and revolt, which appears in the text through the stylistic transgression of the established linguistic rules, and the theme of rebellion against moral values in general. The academic world represents for Bukowski a conformist system, oppressive and threatening for the writer. In the Bukowskian philosophy, the literary critique and the academic world correspond to the Freudian Superego, in charge to censor the information coming from the Id, that is to say from the artist, who is expressing the repressed in a symptomatic way. Verbalization being a liberating act, the work of art has therefore a liberating function upon the creator as well as the reader. The often vehement attacks of the critique regarding Bukowski's work did not slow down his book sales and maybe even contributed to their commercial success. Bukowski has indeed become a cultural icon of the counter-culture. Chinaski is aware of being in opposition to the conservative moral values when he declares with sarcasm and cynicism: "My enemies are the source of half my income. They hate me so much that it becomes a subliminal love affair." In a paradoxical way, the bad criticism itself validates the work of Bukowski, assuring at the same time his publicity. Announcing the attitude and marketing strategy of the punk movement, Bukowski affirms his rejection of culture, which allows him to be crowned king of counter-culture and to be transformed into a product of mass culture. Bukowski has become the most widely read poet in the world and will certainly remain a very popular author since the sales of his books continued growing year after year since his death, in 1994. Bukowski is loved for his vulgarity and idolized for being a brave guerilla fighter whose plans would be to dynamite the literary "artsy-fartsy" establishment. This of course only constitutes the façade, the surface of Bukowski's work, which most readers – lovers or haters – consider the substance. The more profound layers of the text are carefully hidden: "the lair of the hunted is / hidden in the last place / you'd ever look / and even if you find it / you won't believe / it's really there / in much the same way / as the average person / will not believe a great painting." Bukowski doesn't give away his sensitivity and his deep emotions to the dilettante reader, for the real meaning of his work transcends rebellion and the desire of transgression. These, just like his use of humor, are nothing but the keys that will open the doors to the real meaning of the text:

> they thought I had guts
> that I had no fear
> but they had it all wrong.
> It was just that I was frightened of
> many more important things.

Abel Debritto
ATOMIC SCRIBBLINGS FROM A MANIAC AGE:
THE ARTWORK OF CHARLES BUKOWSKI

BY 1966, CHARLES BUKOWSKI'S WORK was featured in so many little magazines that he was soon to be hailed as a "spiritual leader" of the so-called mimeograph revolution that was taking place across the United States. His poetry was unabashedly promoted in hundreds of alternative periodicals, which eventually earned him the indisputable honor of being the most published author of the decade. Shortly before the "mimeo" revolution reached its peak, Bukowski began to work on an unusual project titled Atomic Scribblings from a Maniac Age. While Bukowski had illustrated some of his previous publications, such as Longshot Pomes for Broke Players, Atomic Scribblings was to be the first book where his artwork would be predominantly showcased, with a few interspersed poems, thus turning the volume into a rara avis in the Bukowski canon.

However, despite Bukowski's intense, passionate involvement in the project, it was finally aborted when the publisher, Wayne Philpot, vanished with Bukowski's drawings in 1966. Philpot, who had printed Bukowski's poetry in his little magazine Border in January 1965, was probably stunned by the quality of the drawings and doodles Bukowski selflessly decorated his lengthy letters with. Philpot requested Bukowski several drawings and, one of them, titled "Sunday Afternoon In Heaven," graced the front cover of Border #2 in April 1965. Bukowski's illustrations had such a vivid impact on Philpot that he immediately prompted him to tackle the book of drawings and poems: "I have a proposition that may... or may not... interest you ... Border Press ... would like to bring out a limited edition of Buk's drawings (black & white) with only a few poems along w/them (4 or 5)" (Davidson, 9 Apr. 1965). Bukowski gladly complied by sending dozens of drawings to Philpot during the ensuing months.

Bukowski was corresponding with several authors and editors at the time, and he discussed the ongoing project with them. As he confided to Canadian poet Al Purdy in June 1965, he had already begun "a book of poems and drawings, mostly drawings, untitled and undone so far, but that I will work up in a couple of months for Border Press" (The B./Purdy Letters 79). Bukowski so enthused about the notion of having his drawings published in book form that he even showed them to Henry Miller in August 1965. Two months later, he declared to Purdy that he was still working on Atomic Scribblings. In another undated letter from Philpot to Bukowski, probably from late

1965, he listed the 15 drawings he had accepted so far for the book: "Easel of a Fanatic with Indigestion," "The Death of Karl Marx," and "Portrait of a Dog Elected to a Senatorial Seat" were the titles of some of the drawings to be published in Atomic Scribblings.

Promotional flyers, order forms and adverts were issued in late 1965. However, in a common, yet infuriating practice among small press and little magazine editors, the project came to nothing without a single explanatory note. Bukowski, who had undergone similar experiences, such as a joint William Corrington/Charles Bukowski chapbook cancelled halfway by Marcus Smith in 1962, suspected that Philpot's artistic enterprise would not be completed, and he remarked as much to Douglas Blazek, who had advertised Atomic Scribblings in Olé in early 1966: "Please do not run any more ads ... this guy does not respond to inquiry and evidently isn't going to publish the thing, yet he's hooking all the $3.50's [retail price] that come in and make me look like a crook" (Gotlieb, 6 July 1966). Almost six months later, in November 1966, Bukowski confirmed his suspicions to Marvin Malone, and in November 1967 he summed up the episode to Allen De Loach, editor of Intrepid, where his work would appear in several issues in the late 60s and early 70s: "I sat up night and day for 3 weeks, drunk, naked, laughing to myself, awakening in the morning ... covered with india ink ... I gave him a title ... Atomic Scribblings Upon a Farting World and mailed the batch to him. I saw ads for the book here and there. I wrote Wayne. No response" ("Letter to De Loach" 105-6). For some unfathomable reason, Bukowski concluded, Philpot burned all the drawings.

However, not all those sketches were destroyed because eleven of them eventually surfaced in 1971 in the second issue of Harrison Street Review, a little magazine edited by John Arnoldy and Lawrence Alton. According to both editors, the drawings were "part of a series in the fifties that were to have been published under the title Photo of a Dogs Heart. Drawings lent by Wayne Philpot" (Bukowski, "Portfolio" 20). Inaccuracies and change of title notwithstanding, Bukowski confirmed to Arnoldy that Philpot had disappeared with his illustrations without further notice: "On Philpot the story is sad ... he dropped out of contact after I'd drawn him up 2 or 3 hundred drawings" (Lilly, 2 June 1971). When asked about Philpot and his lending the drawings to the magazine, Arnoldy's reply did not cast light on a rather unusual chain of events: "He said his name was Wayne Philpot and he had a cache of drawings by Charles Bukowski that he wanted to donate to Harrison Street Review. We thanked him ... we never saw him again or learned how he had come into possession of the drawings" (Arnoldy). At any rate, even if two or three hundred illustrations had been destroyed or lost, Bukowski was elated to see them in print. Bukowski had always believed that his drawings and Thurberesque doodles were as valid an art form as any, and the fact that he attended art classes in late 1956 and early 1957 at Los Angeles City College corroborates his passion for painting. Despite the five year delay, it is undeniable that Bukowski was delighted to learn that some of the Atomic Scribblings drawings had been finally made available to the public.

Editors and publishers alike acknowledged Bukowski's art by printing his drawings in their publications. As early as 1946-47, Whit Burnett, the legendary editor of the prestigious Story magazine, urged him on several occasions to submit more sketches for consideration. Bukowski explained to Burnett that he did not have "any other pen sketches, without stories, right now. Matrix took the only one I did that way" (Princeton, 27 Apr. 1947). Indeed, Matrix had reproduced a somewhat uncommon Bukowski drawing to illustrate his short-story "The Reason Behind Reason," published in the summer of 1946 issue. Even though Burnett did not recall having published him in Story, much to Bukowski's chagrin, he was especially fond of his sketches, always mentioning them in glowing terms: "It was pleasant to hear from you again, and particularly to see your wonderful drawings" (Princeton, 29 March 1952). Since all the short-stories from the mid to late 40s were hand-printed, Bukowski illustrated them lavishly in order to highlight them, as he noted in 1953 to Caresse Crosby, Portfolio editor. While he claimed that he had destroyed all the rejected short-stories from that period, he occasionally requested some of them to be returned since he was prouder of the drawings than of the stories themselves. In 1948, he asked Burnett to send back the short-story "A Kind, Understanding Face" because the drawings "came out especially well" (Princeton, Nov. 1948).

Bukowski's letters were embellished with drawings as well, and the center sections and front covers of the Black Sparrow Press volumes of selected correspondence evidence their relevance. In some singular cases, as in a 1946 letter to Crosby, the illustrations became stories in themselves, where Bukowski used words as mere captions. It was an art form that he successfully cultivated in the 70s, when he conceived several cartoon strips for underground newspapers. The drawings from the 1946 letter to Crosby bear a striking resemblance to the comic strips featured in Los Angeles Free Press almost three decades later. Cartoons had always been yet another outlet for Bukowski's prolific output, and not only in letter form. He submitted a group of them to a mainstream magazine in the mid to late 50s, most probably when he was taking art classes at Los Angeles City College with Fry. As he explained to William Corrington:

Fry once egged me on to make a bunch of cartoons with captions, the joke bit, and I stayed up all night, drinking and making these cartoons, laughing at my own madness ... I mailed [them] to either the New Yorker or Esquire ... I wrote about my 45 cartoons and they never came back. 'No such item rec. from you,' wrote back some editor ... [Then] I came across one of my largest no-caption drawings (I mean, the idea of it, it was not my drawing) upon the front cover of the New Yorker, then, I knew I'd had it. (Centenary, Apr. 1962)

Years later, when he was feverishly corresponding with Sheri Martinelli in the very early 60s, she published his first cartoon strip ever in the Anagogic & Paideumic Review #6 (Sept. 1961). The untitled series was made up of nine drawings with relatively long, humorous captions, the last of which showed Ezra Pound and Aldous Huxley embroiled in a heated discussion.

Critics realized that editors appreciated Bukowski's art since they regularly published his drawings and doodles in their magazines and chapbooks. As early as 1970, bibliographer Sanford Dorbin remarked that Bukowski's Poems and Drawings "included three of his drawings. Since then a number of his books as well as some of his newspaper and magazine appearances have featured his own art work" ("Little Mag," 24). Indeed, besides the unusual illustration printed in Matrix in 1946 and the cartoon strip reproduced in the Anagogic & Paideumic Review in 1961, Bukowski's drawings appeared on the front cover and throughout his second chapbook, Longshot Pomes for Broke Players (1961), in It Catches My Heart in Its Hands (1963), where they illustrated poems such as "Old Man, Dead in a Room" or "The Tragedy of the Leaves," on the front cover of Border #2 (1965), in several Open City issues (1967-69), including a captionless cartoon titled "The Horseplayer" (1967), or in the first issue of Open City's literary insert, Renaissance (1968), featuring a series of illustrations dedicated to his daughter Marina.

His artwork was similarly showcased in underground newspapers, little magazines and small press publications in the ensuing decades. The most remarkable case was Los Angeles Free Press, where his fiction and poetry were championed in over 200 issues, most of them displaying his illustrations as well as several comic strips titled "The Adventures of Clarence Hiram Sweetmeat" that Black Sparrow Press and Paget Press subsequently issued as Dear Mr. Bukowski (1979) and The Day It Snowed in L.A. (1986). Bukowski seemed to effortlessly produce so many "Clarence Hiram" cartoons that in the early 80s, when he was no longer contributing to the Los Angeles Free Press, he suggested to the High Times editors, who were publishing Bukowski's short-stories on a monthly basis, that he could revive those cartoons for their magazine, but the project never crystallized (Sloman, Nov. 1982). The "littles," however, did promote his art, which appeared in the main pages of literally hundreds of issues and even on the front cover of alternative publications such as The Sunset Palms Hotel (1974), The Moment (1990) or the New Censorship (1991), to name a few.

Likewise, booksellers used Bukowski's drawings to illustrate their catalogues, hence increasing their value. Jeffrey Weinberg recalls that Bukowski was "cooperative, friendly and humble" and selflessly sent him a poem and several drawings for Under the Influence, a Bukowski-only catalogue released in 1984. Three years later, in spite of the success brought about by the movie Barfly, Bukowski was generous enough to give away his artwork to a bookseller in Canada: "I decided to produce a list of my Bukowski holdings for collectors, inviting Hank to contribute a cover drawing. He doodled up four submissions – of which I used two." Editors and publishers alike valued Bukowski's art throughout his career by printing his unmistakable drawings and doodles or, as in the case of Black Sparrow Press or Loujon Press, by selling limited editions of his books with unique paintings that turned them into highly-priced collectibles over time.

Indeed, John Martin, Bukowski's longtime publisher and editor at Black Sparrow Press, realized from the very onset of their "unholy alliance" that Bukowski's art was financially profitable: ninety original drawings by Bukowski were tipped-in in the limited edition of their first lengthy literary venture, At Terror Street and Agony Way (1968), which was soon to become a much coveted possession by collectors. Shortly before The Days Run Away Like Wild Horses Over the Hills was released in late 1969, Martin asked Bukowski to produce fifty illustrations for the signed, numbered edition, hardbound in boards, of the first comprehensive bibliography of his work, A Bibliography of Charles Bukowski (1969). Although painting was apparently the easiest art form for Bukowski, as recounted in the short-story "East Hollywood: The New Paris," he occasionally complained about the fact that Martin commissioned him dozens of illustrations for each new book, as if they were strictly compulsory. Moreover, he was acutely aware of Martin's ulterior motives: "I threw 30 paintings in the garbage and Martin just about killed me ... He claims I threw away 2 or 3 grand. Now, Sanford, you know I didn't throw away 2 or 3 grand, I threw away some paintings that didn't look good to me," he explained to his bibliographer in 1970 (Dorbin, "Unpublished," 16 Apr.

1970) –the next day he sent a similar letter to poet and friend Harold Norse, mocking Martin's financial concerns. Even though Martin's businesslike vision of his art, where paintings equated with easy money, seemed to disappoint Bukowski, he continued to duly create hundreds of illustrations and drawings for Black Sparrow Press up until his death in 1994. Painting was, ultimately, a compulsion tantamount to writing, a most incurable disease he adamantly refused to fight against.

WORKS CITED

Arnoldy, John. "Drawings." E-mail to the author. 8 Feb. 2009.

Bukowski, Charles. The Bukowski/Purdy Letters 1966-1974. Ed. Seamus Cooney. Sutton West & Santa Barbara: The Paget Press, 1983.

—. "Letter to De Loach." Late Nov. 1967. All's Normal Here. A Charles Bukowski Primer. Ed. Loss Pequeño Glazier. Fremont, CA: Rudy Duck Press, 1985. 104-7.

—. "Portfolio." Harrison Street Review 2 (1971): 20-24.

Centenary: John William Corrington Papers & Manuscripts (Box 30A), Centenary College, Magale Memorial Library, Shreveport, Louisiana.

Davidson: Charles Bukowski Papers. Mss 12. Department of Special Collections, Davidson Library, University of California, Santa Barbara.

Dorbin, Sanford. "Charles Bukowski and the Little Mag/Small Press Movement." Soundings: Collections of the University Library 2.1 (May 1970): 17-32.

—. Unpublished correspondence made available to the author.

Drumbolis, Nicky. Letter to the author. 27 Aug, 2007.

Gotlieb: Richards Manuscript Collection, Howard Gotlieb Archival Research Center, Boston University.

Lilly: American Literature mss., Lilly Library, Indiana University, Bloomington, Indiana.

Princeton: Archives of Story Magazine and Story Press (Box 19, Folder 13; Box 47, Folder 5, and Box 53, Folder 39); Department of Rare Books and Special Collections, Princeton University Library, Princeton, New Jersey.

Sloman, Larry. Unpublished correspondence made available to the author.

Weinberg, Jeffrey. E-mail to the author. 31 Mar. 2010.

Michael Basinski
LIFE AND DEATH IN CHARLES BUKOWSKI'S
THE LAST NIGHT OF THE EARTH POEMS

THE LAST NIGHT OF THE EARTH POEMS was the last book of poetry that Charles Bukowski published before his death in 1994 at the age of 73. It is more than 400 pages long and collects over 150 poems. As Bukowski grew older and became sedate, stationary and reflective, his literary production experientially grew. The poems in *The Last Night of the Earth Poems* present Bukowski's complex preoccupations and opinions written at the culmination of his imagination's evolution. Poetry for Charles Bukowski was a philosophical, intellectual and emotional daybook or journal where themes were repeated and examined from many varied, sometimes extreme and contradictory, perspectives. In *The Last Night of the Earth Poems* there are poems of gratitude and homage, Bukowski's heroes are named and their qualities defined, and love takes the place of emotional confrontation with the wildly erotic muse/whore of Bukowski's earlier poetry.

As in his other books Bukowski confronts death in *The Last Night of the Earth Poems*. It is not the death that he toyed with during his early man-hood and middle-life. It is not the death he challenged on skid row. In *The Last Night of the Earth Poems* the death that Bukowski confronts in his own mortality. By the late 1980s Bukowski's health was in decline. To cope with his eventual death, to fortify his emotions and to give meaning to his long and sometimes chaotic life, Bukowski searched his imagination and memory. He found that what made life worth enduring was writing and the art of acknowledged masters, a philosophy based on extreme convictions and individualism, friends and heroes, and love. However, it was the act of writing, Bukowski's creative energy, which emerged as the principal driving force in his life. Each day he was refreshed by writing. Each day he was born anew. As literal death stalked Bukowski, he was constantly reborn and his writing was his rebirth. He discovered it was creative life that held death at bay. This discovery and Bukowski's acknowledgement of it reveals that Charles Bukowski as a poet was engaged very much in the great natural cycles of the seasons and, therefore, the cosmos. As a resolution to his eventual death, Bukowski recognized himself as part of the cosmic whole. The poems in *The Last Night of the Earth Poems* temper and balance the extremes that were the hallmarks of his literary career. Life and death in *The Last Night of the Earth Poems* are in balance.

In his poem Ill Bukowski wrote, "back in bed you consider death again and find/ the same thing: the closer you get to it/ the less forbidding it/ becomes." In Mugged he wrote, "much about dying is getting ready./ the tiger walks through my dreams." His last book's title *The Last Night of the Earth Poems* attests to Bukowski's belief that the poems he was writing were to be among his last. Self-centered, Bukowski was the earth, the world and it was night, the end. But the earth is not a masculine image. The earth is feminine and evokes the generative spirit, which exists in the dark. What follows the falling of night, the darkness, is the approaching dawn or rebirth and a celebration of creativity or creative fecundity. The first poem of the book, Jam, comments on the state of humanity, of which Bukowski was a part. He wrote, "we were like some last, vast/ final dinosaur/ crawling feebly home somewhere, somehow/ maybe/ to/ die." This is bleak. This is the end. This poem foreshadows the death of all of society. The dinosaur image of society and collective death is again addressed in the poem Dinosauria, We, which opens the final section of the book. In the poem Mrs. Death laughs and bodies rot. Decay is upon society and the world. But out of the decay, Bukowski writes, "born out of that.// the sun still hidden there// awaiting the next chapter." The notion of regeneration and rebirth exists at the conclusion of Dinasauria, We. Regeneration springs from destruction and day follows night.

The past in Bukowski's imagination was a warehouse of poetic raw materials. Bukowski's father, a bitterly frustrated, ignorant and angry man is an often recalled monster. The supper table is a stage where his ugliness was repeatedly exhibited. The image of his father was with Bukowski throughout his decades of writing. In 1957 Bukowski's published a poem called My Father. In it he wrote, "My father liked rules and the hard way./ He spoke of responsibilities and laws/ and things that just had to be done./ A Man must work, a man must eat." Bukowski's father consumes. In the poem Dinner, 1933, from *The Last Night of the Earth Poems*, Bukowski wrote, "when my father ate/ his lips became/ greasy/ with food." And in the poem They Don't Eat Like Us, he wrote, " my father eating.// his ears moved.// he munched with great vigor." And later in that poem Bukowski writes, "watching him eat brought on the darkness." A typical dinner scenes was portrayed in a short story called Love, Love, Love, published in 1946. In the story Bukowski wrote,

"Do you want some more potatoes?"

"No."
"More meat?"
"No."
"More Celery?"
"No."
"Do you want some more coffee?"
"No."
"More Peas?"
"No."
"How about some bread?"
"No. NO! Goddamn it, if I want anything, I'll ask for it!"
"Now what's the matter with you?" yells my father.

His father represents an evil power, an all consuming Moloch. He was representative of the worst in individuals and society. He was a destructive, consuming figure. In the poem They Are Everywhere Bukowski wrote, "I have seen a/ thousand/ fathers,/ ten thousand/ fathers/ wasting their lives/ in hatred,/tossing their lives/ into the/ cesspool/ and/ ranting/ on."

In direct opposition to his father, consuming father images and all the fathers of the world were the artists, composers, and rebels with bright eyes. In *The Last Night of the Earth Poems* the artist heroes are Gertrude Stein, Huxley, Hamsun, Marlin Brando, Wagner, Celine, E. E. Cummings, Hemingway, Faulkner, Rossini, Shostakovich and others. These heroes represent the world of wonder and beauty and creativity, as opposed to rude, stagnant death. In the poem Dinner, 1933, Bukowski wrote from the perspective of a small boy, "out there,/ out there/ in another world/ I didn't/ live/ in." Bukowski sought the world of art, which was a world as far away form his reality as he could imagine. In the poem Them and Us Bukowski wrote about a party at the house of his parents where the guests included Hemingway, T.S. Eliot, Pound and others. Bukowski wrote, 'and he," my father pointed to me,/ 'wants to be like them!'// 'is that true? my mother asked.// 'not like them,' I said, 'but of/ them. Bukowski located life in creativity and like his heroes donned the mask of the artist.

To fortify himself, to gather strength and vigor and to resist death Bukowski searched his past, as he had always done, to locate romantic images that glorified his perspective. The Poem a Job is representative. In this poem Bukowski recalls a long brutalizing day of manual, yet manly and heroic labor. He unloads boxcars of frozen fish. He wrote, "the night came/ on and you flickered/ the headlights/ on// and the world was/ good enough,/ right/ then." There was a light in the dark. And again in the poem Those Mornings he glorified his life and the endless mornings in which he confronted existence, finding calm in the midst of ugliness. Bukowski wrote in the poem Those Mornings "I walked to work as the sun/ came up hot/ and the whores slept/ like babies." In Bukowski's poetry whores represent chaotic unstable emotional and sexual relationships. Sex is the most chaotic of human drives. To have the whores asleep in Those Morning is to master chaos. Bukowski was the dominant, procreative, male sun.

Bukowski wrote about his ailments. In his poem "D" Bukowski had a cancerous growth removed and in the poem Upon This Time, it was tuberculosis that plagued him. In his poem Ill it was an unnamed contagious disease. His illnesses and his old age were undeniable. He realized that his death was upon him. In his poem The Creative Act, he wrote, "this life dancing in front of/ Mrs. Death." There is nothing, even vaguely, erotic about Mrs. Death, the same Mrs. Death who laughs in Dinosauria, We. She is not a whore/muse. She was simply death waiting. However, in Death Is Smoking My Cigars Bukowski personified death as male, He wrote, "Well, death says, as he walks by,/ I'm going to get you anyhow. In his poem The Pack, Bukowski wrote about death as a pack of dogs, "they are circling me/ in this room." But more than a male or female personification of death, death was a specter stalking Charles Bukowski. It was this specter that Bukowski waits for in the poem In The Shadow of the Rose. Bukowski wrote, "slide a fresh clip into the/ automatic,/ turn out the lights and/ wait." Bukowski sensed, in the shadow of the allegorical rose, that he could defeat or at least keep death at a distance. He would not accept his fate passively. The rose, his writing, his artistic powers, his poetry would slow death's onslaught. To avoid death Bukowski embraced and was embraced by the creative, generative female force.

There is very little actual sexual contact in *The Last Night of the Earth Poems*. Bukowski avoids it in his imagination. If Bukowski accepts the whore as muse his creative and poetic energy is only chaotic and dark. He must then surrender to death and die because the erotic, the unbridled passion of Eros, is death. Death is something that Bukowski flatly rejects in *The Last Night of the Earth Poems* In the poem Freaky Time Bukowski tosses away a pack of cigarette's labeled DEATH, which he acquired in a sleazy bar from a whore who he recognizes as death. He rejects her and rejects death. As he does this he opens himself to accepting love, the generative as a stable form of positive passion.

The love poems, almost completely sentimental love poems, which appear in *The Last Night of the Earth Poems* are a result of Bukowski balancing his darkness and light, life and death and the erotic and the sublime extremes. Bukowski's love poems, like Peace and Confession, allow Bukowski to fully reveal his mythopoetic self. He is totally involved in the cycles of life. This is no stunning surprise for the heroic poet/character Henry Chinaski always survived and thrived in the midst of life and death and was somehow very much part of both.

The true nature of Bukowski's poetry has always haunted his literary career. Bukowski's poetry was always full of obtuse confrontation. In this collection, after a lifetime of orgy in words and ideas and a strictly belligerent stance, Bukowski presents the poem The Bluebird. In the poem Bukowski wrote, "There's a bluebird in my heart that/ wants to get out/ but I'm too clever, I only let him out/ at night sometimes/ when everybody's asleep." At the beginning of his book It Catches My Heart in Its Hands he wrote, "small birds who go/ the way of cats sing/ on inside my head." The song of this dead bird singing in Bukowski's imagination is truly the romantic soul that Bukowski cleverly kept caged throughout his literary career and only revealed in tiny glimpses, which are forgotten in the midst of bar room brawls and binges. This self is finally revealed in Bukowski's poem The Confession, the most obvious love poem in the collection. The final two lines of the poem are, "I love/ you." In this poem there is bucolic love, which is the opposite of sexual chaos. Accepting death, or confronting his own death, Bukowski accepts life without the duress of the overwhelming wildly erotic nature of life. Accepting life forces death to linger in the shadows, it pushes death away. For example in the poem Peace, Bukowski keeps death waiting while he casually dines intimately in a small cafe. He wrote, "there is no war/ there is no hell" and as the middle-aged couple relax after their dinner, Bukowski wrote, "the streets outside/ flower/ in the/ night."

Non-sexual or pastoral white love is non-violent and this circumstance allows Bukowski to generate reams of poetry. Love and creativity grant Bukowski life. The act of creation is a positive life affirmation and as Bukowski each day faced his approaching death he wrote more and more and was able to hold death at bay. He did not accomplish this with a gun or a bottle or a whore, but with the rose of life, love and creativity manifested as poetry, which allowed him to meld with the essence of the great cycles of day and night, light and dark and life and death.

Writing was Charles Bukowski's salvation. Throughout his life his identity was anchored by the word. In the poem The Creative Act, Bukowski revealed that it was in fact his writing that was the sole purpose in life. He wrote, "for the 5th of July/ for the fish in the tank/ for the old man in room 9/ for the cat on the fence// for yourself." And in the poem Death is Smoking My Cigars, he wrote, "I just wanted to get the word/ down;/ fame, money, didn't matter." And again in the poem Only One Cervantes, Bukowski wrote, "writing has been my fountain/ of youth/ my whore,/ my love,/ my gamble." And all of this writing goes on in the face of death. For example, he wrote in the poem Are You Drinking?, "so here I am/ propped against my pillows/ again.// just an old guy/ just and old writer/ with a yellow/ notebook.// something is/ walking across the/ floor/ toward/ me." And again in the poem The Creative Act, perhaps the most telling poem in this collection, he wrote, "this life dancing in front of / Mrs. Death." Here death, as before noted, is a non-erotic female. She is the Great Mother. Earth cradles her mythical hero. It is in the arms of death that the creative act (birth) is balanced and so Bukowski's poetry enters the eternal realm of art. Bukowski wrote in the poem No More, No Less, "each day is still a/ hammer,/ a flower." All is balanced and in harmony as dictated by the eternal order of nature in the universe.

D.A. Pratt
WHO GETS TO READ BUKOWSKI?

I RECENTLY GAVE A YOUNG WOMAN a book of Charles Bukowski's poetry. I went to some effort to do this, since going to the local bookstore and picking up a recent Ecco reprint just wasn't going to be good enough in my mind. Let's face it: in the second decade of the twenty-first century, it is difficult to experience Bukowski in the way that his "front-line fans" did while he was alive. Difficult? Try impossible! Nevertheless, when I decided to give a book of Bukowski's poetry to one of the servers in her early 20s at my favourite bar, I opted to get for her a used copy of a Black Sparrow Press edition of Love is a Dog from Hell so that she would have, at the very least, a chance to experience some sense of how holding a book by Bukowski would have felt some years ago. Of course, one cannot really recreate this feeling but I thought it was important to make the effort. When I gave it to her, she noted that it was an old book – something she seemed to appreciate ...

The undertaking led me to again ask myself a question that has been with me for some time: in the early twenty-first century, who gets to read Bukowski? The question applies especially to his poetry. Since "anyone and everyone" is naturally one possible answer to this question, given the availability of the Ecco reprints of many of the Black Sparrow Press editions, one has to look for the nuances in the enquiry to get at the essence of the question. One variation of the theme is this enquiry: does someone just starting to read Bukowski today, as we get ever closer to the twentieth anniversary of his death in 1994, have any real chance to experience Bukowski's poetry in a way that comes even close to how many of his first readers did? What are the roadblocks to doing this? And what are there steps to allowing, say, a young person to experience Bukowski as he should be experienced? The efforts I made to give one person an older copy of a book of poetry illustrates the whole damn thing – after all, I could have directed her to our local bookstore, which indeed has several Bukowski titles in its poetry section as well as its fiction section.

The first roadblock these days to anyone entering and really "getting at" Bukowski's work is the number of posthumous collections of poetry. No one should begin reading Bukowski's poetry by reading one of the "original" titles published posthumously. That would not be fair to both the new reader and Bukowski himself. Therefore, if we are introducing Bukowski to new readers, we cannot simply direct them to a local bookstore – the danger of starting with one of those posthumous poetry books is far too real.

Parenthetically, the real challenge in "getting into Bukowski's writing" in the early twenty-first century is his poetry. Access to Bukowski's prose is much easier: his novels are in print (generally as Ecco reprints) and there have been some recent collections of his shorter prose that, I feel, serve Bukowski very well. Of course, it is saddening that his marvelously entitled collection Erections, Ejaculations, Exhibitions and General Tales of Ordinary Madness is now only readily available in reprints that both divide the collection and lose the original dedication to Linda King. Nevertheless, a young reader today definitely has a good shot at reading much of Bukowski's prose. The real question is about getting the right kind of access to his poetry.

ELEVATOR

If the young woman to whom I have given one of Bukowski's books of poetry were to want to read more, where should she turn? I've already said 'no' to the posthumous books of poetry (yes, they surely have their moments but, to me, they seem soul-less – I've been adding them to my Bukowski collection but without much enthusiasm). Given the chance, I actually would like to point her toward one particular period of his writing. In saying this, I believe that Bukowski's works can be divided into four periods, which (in turn) create four groups of books. They are:

(1) The publications prior to Notes of a Dirty Old Man – in essence, the ten works that Black Sparrow Press often listed as appearing before 1969;

(2) Those works published between 1969 and 1979 inclusive – this period extends from Notes of a Dirty Old Man to Women, with the publications in 1979 also thrown in (there are no publications in 1980);

(3) The works published after 1980 up until his death in 1994

– this period begins with the 1981 publication of Dangling in the Tournefortia and ends with the 1994 publication of Pulp; and

(4) The works published after his death.

Regardless of how we describe these four periods, I find myself wanting to ensure that a young reader of Bukowski's poetry actually stays away from the latter two when beginning to plunge into Bukowski's poetry. Speaking personally, my own interest in Bukowski begins to wane whenever I dip into the books published after the second period (I have similar feelings about the writings of Henry Miller – the books he wrote after the book-length essay "The World of Sex" are not up to his earlier efforts in my eyes). Therefore, I would tend to want to direct any young reader of Bukowski toward books from the first two periods – and herein is the problem: these days, who really gets to read the earliest books by Bukowski?

The first period (based upon lists that appeared in many publications of the Black Sparrow Press – by the way these lists generously included titles not published by John Martin's press) includes the following:

TITLE	YEAR
1— Flower, Fist and Bestial Wail	1960
2— Longshot Pomes for Broke Players	1962
3— Run with the Hunted	1962
4— It Catches My Heart in Its Hands	1963
5— Crucifix in a Deathhand	1965
6— Cold Dogs in the Courtyard	1965
7— Confessions of a Man Insane Enough to Live with Beasts	1965
8— All the Assholes in the World and Mine	1966
9— At Terror Street and Agony Way	1968
10— Poems Written Before Jumping out of an 8 Story Window	1968

As a footnote to this list, I would like to note that it is a curious selection by the editors of the Black Sparrow Press. The titles vary in both size and what I will label as "production values". Two of these items (numbers 7 and 8) represent single stories that indeed appeared as small but separate items. The first book is quite "slim" (just 16 poems) whereas the two published by Jon and Louise Webb (numbers 4 and 5) are major undertakings, to put it mildly.

What chance does the young woman to whom I gave one of Bukowski's books have of ever reading any of these early titles? Have you seen the prices being asked for copies of these early titles on ABE, the online book-selling site I access most of the time when looking for the odd and the old? The young woman I've been mentioning is a university student who works part-time as a server in my favourite bar. It's darn difficult to imagine that she could afford to purchase any of the titles in the early group (it's stretching things to imagine that I can afford to purchase these titles).

Admittedly, some (many?) of the poems in these books are available elsewhere, in some of the collections of selected poetry (for example, The Roominghouse Madrigals, published in 1988, presents a selection of early poetry from the years 1946 to 1966). With some effort, one can actually read all the poems of Bukowski's first book – the effort includes accessing Bukowski.net to get the one poem from that first chapbook that has not been reprinted elsewhere. However, this is not true for the other poetry collections in the "early Bukowski".

So who gets to read the "early Bukowski" these days? Only those who already own copies of the earliest books? Those who have the financial resources to pay the high prices being asked for these items? Bukowski himself might have thought that his earliest loyal readers deserve this privilege. On the other hand, would Bukowski be happy with the idea that only the wealthy, who are actually interested in books as books, now be the ones to get to read his earliest poetry as it was presented in those early books? I like to think that he would want other people to have the chance to see them.

Someday, these books will be reprinted so that readers can read the poems as they originally appeared (and not just in selections that are dependent on various editors). In the meantime, I am asking, "Who gets to read Bukowski in the early twenty-first century?"

Ann Menebroker
WHEN THE ODDS ARE 99 TO ONE

I HAPPENED TO FALL IN LOVE with poetry for no known reason. It was just there. It was the mystery for me. Albert Einstein wrote it best:

> *The most beautiful experience we can have is the mysterious. It is the fundamental emotion that stands at the cradle of true art and true science.*

I starting writing young and I wrote a lot of lousy poems. But along the way I ran into those who would become my mentors. Among them were Walt Whitman, Emily Dickinson, Edna St. Vincent Millay, Thomas Merton, e e cummings, and many more. My own peers also illuminated and challenged me. By the time I was sending work out, it was a horse race. I hadn't been trained for this and I never won a big race, but my heart was in it, and has been all these years. When I had been publishing awhile, three poet's work hit me and changed me. These three were Sylvia Plath, Anne Sexton and Charles Bukowski.

What they did was start a fire under me and jockeyed me into a position on the inside rail. It didn't matter what position I came in on; it was just being there at all, focusing on the track.

Charles Bukowski had something special. He was unique, a man bursting with words and reflections, an assurance of himself He knew where the power was, where the words should fall, when few he saw around him were doing it, feeling it, understanding it. People began coming to him for answers because he seemed to live under his own skin, feel his own pulse, take chances and not bow to fear, or give food to it. Instead he walked all over it, sat on it, made lunchmeat out of it and ate it. Better yet, he was alive. Plath had committed suicide, and in the early 1970s, Sexton followed suit. Bukowski went on for twenty more years after Sexton. He didn't commit suicide. He just got old and sick and died.

He's been gone ten years since his death on March 9, 1994. Books explore his personality, his writing, his attraction to so many people. Poets continue to try and write like him, be like him. Whether you accepted him as a great poet or not, his appeal and fascination was real. His dark side grabbed at our daily imagination. His mark on literary history is firmly entrenched. After ten years his poems are still being published posthumously. More biographies. More stories. More about him than you'd ever want or need to know. The curiosity remains high. The devotion to his writing remains strong.

Charles "Hank" Bukowski probably knew who he was best of all. His wife, Linda, knew him almost as well, and John Martin, his publisher of many years through Black Sparrow Press, knew the writer and the man as an editor and friend.

With all of the material out on him, anyone can feel that they knew him a little better . If you read his poems and his novels and short stories, you knew him even better.

If you watched him coming up from the beginning, you felt something different was happening. Some of the editors knew it back then. Women were already starting to get goofy over him. Poets were finding a way to his apartment to drink with him. He just kept doing what he did.

He didn't believe he was going to go anywhere big, not at first. He was middle-aged when he began to take hold in the underground literary world, and over in Europe. The academics dismissed him. His fans praised him.

But all along he kept writing. He dismissed what was being said about him. He was doing what he wanted. When it was over, he left a silent race track. The party was over, baby, and he'd had a good run.

He wrote in the poem Snow White,

> the slow retreat, no trumpets here, backing into it,
> you can only wonder, did you put up a good fight?
>
> or was it all just
> a stupid joke?
>
> we can only hope not.

Shortly after he died, I wrote two poems for him, and said goodbye.I continue to read his work. I continue to feel his presence.

mid nov. 1982

Hello Norman ##########Olson:

I usually type when drunk so forgive typing.

Thanks the words on HAM.

Like you must guess I've done the factory trip myself, in fact in 1970 was still working a shit job. Maybe 12 years of playing at writer has made me lose some contact with the actuality of what happens to most. Like I used to fight for a job I didn't even want. The women I lived with never quite understood this ####mix-up in functionals.

I write because I have to. There's no other choice.

But #if I feel anything about the aftermath of having written while drinking what I like are the letters I get from people in madhouses, jails and factories, ####people who somehow know that what I'm saying is what occurs to most of them, I like that somehow, I allow myself a momentary proudness, then forget it. Because when you get proud you ######forget whatever there is.

Whenever I hear from a college professor I know that I'm not hearing from anywhere.

I take it you must work for some joint that pushes for Paradise in the Pacific. What shit, what shuck. Last place I'd want to be is on some overpriced Hawaaian Island getting taken on the dream.

The best place to be is where you are with the door locked and plenty to drink and with nobody to fuck you over.

o.k., luck to you,

yrs,

C.Bukowski

BIOS

JAY ALAMARES lives in Tennessee. At one time he was a staff writer for the *LUMMOX Journal*. He has been published in numerous magazines, including SIC, Report to Hell; has two chapbooks and was one of the original participants in **Last Call: A Legacy of Madness** (published in 1994 by *Vinegar Hill Press* and *LUMMOX Press*).

RD ARMSTRONG edited and published the *LUMMOX Journal* (1995 to 2006). In addition to that, he publishes the Little Red Book series (in which a number of these writers have appeared). His own work has been published in over 200 magazines and E-zines. His *LUMMOX Press* continues to publish outstanding collections and anthologies of poetry & prose. He has 19 books of poetry, including his latest **E/OR —Living Amongst the Mangled** (available from www.lummoxpress.com).

MICHAEL BASINSKI is the Curator of The Poetry Collection, State University of New York at Buffalo. He has published 29 books of poetry including his most recent: **Poems Popeye Papyrus** by *Slack Buddha Press*.

JOY BUCKLEY lives in Southern California and spent many years in Venice, CA where she hobnobbed with the likes of Tony Scibella and the Venice Beats.

The poetry of PRIS CAMPBELL has appeared in such journals as *Chiron Review, Main Street Rag, Boxcar Poetry Review, The Dead Mule,* and *Wild Goose Review.* She has published six collections of poetry; most recently: **Sea Trails** by *LUMMOX Press*, **The Nature of Attraction**, with Scott Owens, by *Main Street Rag Press*, and **Paul Newman Blues** by *Full of Crow Press*. A former Clinical Psychologist, she was sidelined by ME/CFS in 1990 and now lives in the greater West Palm Beach with her husband.

ALAN CATLIN has published dozens of books of poetry and prose. His latest book is **"Near Death in the Afternoon on Becker Street"** from *March Street Press* who will also bring out his **"Desolation Row Revisited"** in 2011.

NEELI CHERKOVSKI is an applauded poet, critic, memoirist and literary biographer. He has written twelve books of poetry, including: **From the Canyon Outward**, the award winning **Leaning Against Time,**

Elegy for Bob Kaufman and **Animal**; two acclaimed biographies, **Bukowski: A Life** and **Ferlinghetti: A Biography**; his book, **Whitman's Wild Children** (a collection of critical memoirs), has become an underground classic. In the late 1960s Cherkovski co-edited the poetry anthology *Laugh Literary and Man the Humping Guns* with Charles Bukowski. Since 1975, Neeli has lived and worked in San Francisco. Currently Neeli is completing an as yet untitled memoir of his life in poetry, a collection of poems on his travels in the Philippines, and a selected poems.

ABEL DEBRITTO is a Bukowski scholar.

ERIC DEJAEGER was born in 1958. He Lives near Charleroi (Belgium). He is fond of Trappist beer. He has had three books and ten chapbooks published since 1996. You can check the front & back covers of his brand new book **Jivarosseries** (June 2004) on http://www.memor.be/livre.asp?livre=140. Co-editor of the tiny (but excellent) mag *Microbe* (rvmicrobe@yahoo.fr) in which he regularly publishes translations from English.

HENRY DENANDER graduated from the Business School at Uppsala University in Sweden, in 1973. For almost 20 years he has worked on the business side of the entertainment industry. His first book, **I Know What She Will Say** with poetry and artwork was published in 2003 by *Bottle of Smoke Press*. His poems and artwork can be seen in numerous poetry magazines, in print and on the web. Some of his paintings were exhibited at The Los Angeles Municipal Art Gallery in 2004. His next book, **Weeks Like This**, will be published in 2004 by *Bottle of Smoke Press*. He lives in Stockholm, Sweden with his wife and young son. His website can be found at www.henrydenander.com

JOHN DORSEY currently resides in Toledo, Ohio. He is the author of several collections of poetry, including **Teaching the Dead to Sing: The Outlaw's Prayer** (*Rose of Sharon Press*, 2006), and **Sodomy is a City in New Jersey** (*American Mettle Books*, 2010). His work has been nominated for the Pushcart Prize.

DOUG DRAIME started publishing in the small press and "underground' newspapers in the late '60's, while living in Los Angeles. Recent chapbooks include, **Slaves of the Harvest** (*Indian Heritage Publishing*, 2002), **Unoccupied Zone** (*Pitchfork Press*, 2004), and **Spleen** (*Poetic Inhalation*), an ebook, due out in September 2004. His diverse range of writing continues to appear in publications world wide. He moved to Oregon in 1981, where he lives with his wife, Carol.

EDWARD FIELD began writing poetry in 1943 during World War II, after a Red Cross worker handed him an anthology of poetry. But it was not until 1963 that his first book, **Stand Up, Friend, With Me**, won the Lamont Award and was published. In 1992, he received a Lambda Award for **Counting Myself Lucky, Selected Poems 1963-1992**. In 1979, he edited the anthology, **A Geography of Poets**, and in 1992 with Gerald Locklin and Charles Stetler, brought out a sequel, **A New Geography of Poets**. He and his partner Neil Derrick, long-time residents of Greenwich Village, have written a best-selling historical novel about the Village, **The Villagers**. Forthcoming from the *U. of Wisconsin Press* are his literary memoirs, **The Man Who Would Marry Susan Sontag, and Other Intimate Literary Portraits of the Bohemian Era**.

MICHAEL C FORD is a baseball fan, a poet and an ambassador for poetry and the history of the small press in SoCal. He has several Baseball CDs, one entitled **Innings** and the other entitled **PLAY BALL** (on *Hen House*) Included in his catalogue of stage plays is a 2-character pastiche which is a 1-act titled **Termite Palace** (paying homage to the demise of a wooden stadium in Pacific Coast League baseball history). His volume of selected work published by *Amaranth Editions* in 1998 attracted a Pulitzer Prize nomination, as was his latest spoken word recording entitled **20th-Century Goodbye**. He has published four books including **The Marilyn Monroe Concerto** (*Pitchfork Press*); **To Kiss The Blood Off Our Hands** (*Ion Drive Publishing*, 2007); and **The Demented Chauffeur & Other Mysteries** (*Ion Drive Publishing*, 2009). He is currently involved in a CD project which will be marketed with the title **FAST FOOD SANITARIUM**.

BILL GAINER is known for the openness of his confessional poetry and is recognized as one of the founding contributors to the modern movement of "After Hours Poetry." Among other awards and recognitions, Gainer is a past winner of the S.F. Beat Museum's Poetry Contest. He is widely published and continues to be a sought after reader. Visit him at billgainer.com.

JASON HARDUNG was born and raised in Wyoming. He now lives at the base of the Rocky Mountains in Ft. Collins, Colorado, soon to be in Los Angeles. His work has been published widely throughout the American underground. It has appeared in *The New York Quarterly,*

Evergreen Review, 3am, Chiron Review, Rip Rap (the Cal State Long Beach literary journal), *Word Riot, Zygote In My Coffee, Monkey Bicycle, Underground Voices, decomP, Thrasher, LUMMOX Journal* and many more. His first full length book of poetry, **The Broken and The Damned** came out on *Epic Rites Press* late 2009. He has been nominated for a Pushcart Prize like everyone else and is a co-editor of the *Matter Journal*. He is scared of happy people and water.

ANDREW HILBERT lives and works in San Antonio, TX.

G.HAGEN-HILL was a regular contributor to *LUMMOX* publications as well as numerous other small press venues. He has since disappeared into the cloud.

DOUG HOLDER is the founder of the *Ibbetson Street Press*. He teaches writing at Bunker Hill Community College in Boston and Endicott College in Beverly, Mass. For the past 30 years he has run poetry groups for psych patients at McLean Hospital—right outside of Boston. His poetry and prose has appeared in *LUMMOX, The Endicott Review, Heeltap, Poetry Motel, Rattle* and others.

BRETTON B. HOLMES: Prior to his foray into writing he worked as a corrections officer, did a stint in the Marine Corps and worked in a psychiatric hospital. While life experiences can be gained through working a job, he'd much rather gain life experiences through unemployment. His new play, **WELTSCHMERZ** will see its World Premiere in Austin, Texas later this year. His play **WATER, WATER, EVERYWHERE** will be seen in Melbourne, Australia in October 2004, and his latest short story **Hyperbolic Doubt** is slated for publication in *Anthology Magazine* in 2005. He lives with his wife and daughter in Texas.

TODD JACKSON is temporarily done with cubicle life. He is currently teaching 3-5 year olds how to write books. Todd is also the Senior Writer, Chief Editor, Lead Engineer, President and Sole Proprietor of *Odd with a T Publishing.* www.oddwitha-T.com

ED JAMIESON, JR. has lived in Southern Calif. for a very long time and has been writing almost as long. His stuff has been published various times in various places. His LRB is called **Digging My Own Grave**.

MICHAEL P LEFANTO lives in Brooklyn, NY. Been published here & there for the past twenty or so years. He's a retired street laborer.

LINDA LERNER lives in New York. She has been published widely in the small press and has a number of chapbooks.

ELLARAINE LOCKIE is a widely published and awarded poet, nonfiction book author and essayist. Her seventh chapbook, **Stroking David's Leg**, was awarded Best Individual Collection for 2010 from *Purple Patch* magazine in England, and her eighth chapbook, **Red for the Funeral**, won the 2010 San Gabriel Poetry Festival Chapbook Contest. Her current chapbook, **Wild as in Familiar**, was a finalist in *Finishing Line Press'* 2011 contest and has been published there. Ellaraine teaches both poetry and papermaking workshops and serves as Poetry Editor for the lifestyles magazine, *Lilipoh*.

GERALD LOCKLIN has three titles with *LUMMOX Press* (among hundreds published in his nearly 40 years as a poet): **Modest Aspirations** (with Beth Wilson), **The Iceberg Theory & Familiarities** (with Patricia Cherin). Please visit www.geraldlocklin.org and/or glocklin@csulb. edu for more info. Even in retirement, he's still teaching one class a semester at California State University, Long Beach.

JOHN MACKER'S latest book is **Underground Sky** (*Indian Hills: Turkey Buzzard Press*, 2010). Forthcoming: Part III of his **"Borderlands"** trilogy: **Disassembled Badlands**. Contributed several poems to Landscape of Memory exhibit, July/Aug, Gerald Peters Gallery, Santa Fe, NM. Previous books include **Woman of the Disturbed Earth, Burroughs At Santo Domingo** and **Wyoming Arcane** among others. Contributed text to Colorado artist Leon Loughridge's book of woodcuts, **Las Montanas de Santa Fe**. Writes from a converted roadhouse on the Santa Fe Trail in northern New Mexico. Recently has contributed poems and short fiction to *Mas Tequila, Malpais Review, Adobe Walls, Tree Killer Ink #10* (Alberta, Canada), *New Mexico Poetry Review, Sin Fronteras (Writers Without Borders), Santa Fe Poetry Review*.

MICHAEL D. MELOAN'S fiction has appeared in *WIRED, BUZZ*, Larry Flynt's *Chic, L.A. Weekly*, and on Joe Frank's NPR program. He is coauthor of the novel **"THE SHROUD,"** and also a *Huffington Post* featured blogger.

ANN MENEBROKER lives and writes from Sacramento, California. A reprint collection of her *Wormwood Review* published poems came out in summer, 2004, from *R.L. Crow Press*. In addition to that the publication (short run) of **Sunscreen in the Fog**, *Bottle of Smoke Press*

2010. And the up coming, **The Measure of Small Gratitudes** coming out of *Kamin Press* in Sweden in the Fall of 2011.

REBECCA MORRISON is a University of California graduate and works as an environmental analyst for UC Davis. She is the editor of eskimopie.net and hosts monthly readings at the Sacramento Poetry Center and the UC Davis Arboretum. Her passions are reading classic novels of all genres, gardening, and nature. She and her husband live in a 100-year-old Arts and Crafts bungalow in Oak Park, Sacramento.

GERALD NICOSIA is best known for his biography of Jack Kerouac, **Memory Babe**. He has also published a big book on the healing of Vietnam veterans, called **Home to War**, as well as several volumes of poetry. This fall, *Viva Editions* will bring out his book **One and Only: The Untold Story of On the Road and of Lu Anne Henderson Cassady**. He is currently working on a biography of black poet and playwright Ntozake Shange for *St. Martin's Press*.

CLAUDIO PARENTELA lives in Catanzaro, Italy and sends his work out to literally hundreds of magazines & websites...here are a few: *Komix.it, Braintwisting, Lo Sciacallo Elettronico, Inguine, Stripburger, Lavirint, Komikaze, The Cherotic R(e)volutionary, Sick Puppy, Malefact, Gordo.it, Lamette, Chance, Que Suerte, Art Life, Pintalo De Verde, ApArte, Evasion, First Class, This Is Magazine, Diesel, Stu Magazine, Crane Magazine, Staplegun, Untergruntblatte, Head Press.* He was a regular contributor to the *LUMMOX Journal*.

D.A. (David) PRATT lives in Regina, Saskatchewan, Canada. While working far too long as a civil servant in taxation policy, he managed to maintain a "common reader" interest in a wide range of world literature, including writers like Henry Miller, Charles Bukowski and Josef Skvorecky. He tells anyone who cares to listen that reading D.H. Lawrence's **Lady Chatterley's Lover** while he was in high school in the 1960s changed everything for him.

IAM RAWKINREC lives in Pittsburg, PA; sometimes works as a blues musician; has had fiction, artwork, and poetry published in literary and commercial magazines including *Chiron Review, The New York Quarterly, Fair Witness, Impetus, The Iconoclast, The Bukowski Review, Poetry Motel* and *Pearl.*

FRANK REARDON is from Boston Mass & has a complete

collection of poetry called **Interstate Chokehold** on *NeoPoiesis Press*, also **The Nirvana Haymaker** due out Jan 2012 from *NeoPoiesis*. Frank is currently locked away in The Badlands of North Dakota working on a novel & gathering rejections.

CHARLES P. RIES lives in Milwaukee, Wisconsin. He has completed a novel based on memory titled, **THE FATHERS WE FIND: The Making of a Humble, Pleasant Boy**. He has published two books of poetry, **Bad Monk: Neither Here Nor There** and **Monje Malo Speaks English** both published by *Four Sep Publications*. His third book of poetry titled, **Odd** will be published by *Pudding House Publications* in 2004. His work was nominated for a 2003 Pushcart Prize by *Anthology*. His poems, poetry reviews and short stories have appeared in over seventy print and electronic publications. He can be reached at charlesr@execpc.com.

C.C. RUSSELL was born in East Liverpool Ohio, grew up in Wheatland Wyoming, attended the University of Wyoming in Laramie, and is currently living in Hicksville New York with his wife, Caroline. He manages a video games store and has previously worked as a hotel clerk, maintenance man, convenience store clerk and d.j. in a small Wyoming bar.

BEN JOHN SMITH is afraid someone will realize he has no idea what is going on, so he puts on a brave face and criticizes himself before others get a chance. He is the founder of the **HORROR SLEAZE TRASH** shenanigans. www.horrorsleazetrash.com

JOAN JOBE SMITH, founding editor of *Pearl* and *Bukowski Review*, prior to receiving an MFA from UCI, worked 7 years, the length of bad luck for breaking a mirror, as a go-go girl late 60s-early 70s, sharing a stage w/Ike & Tina Turner, Goldie Hawn, Jim Morrison and Dick Dale. Her latest collection, **SEQUIN SOUL**, was produced by *Chance Press*.

MENDE SMITH is a single mom.

RICK SMITH is a clinical psychologist specializing in brain damage and domestic violence. He writes and plays harmonica for **The Mescal Sheiks** (see mescalsheiks.com) and published widely in small press journals such as *Water-Stone, Lungfull!, Blueline, OnTheBus, New Letters* and *Chaffey Review*. He has two books out with *LUMMOX Press*: **The Wren Notebook** (2000) and **Hard Landing** (2010).

JOE SPEER was co-editor of *Beatlick News* (with Pamela Hirst), producer of **Speer Presents**—a television program created on the road and mailed back to the station. In Feb. of 2011, Joe passed away suddenly. His novel **Pages: A Memoir of the 1960's**, is available at the www.beatlick.com site. Like RD, Joe had been reading Buk since 1969. Now Joe's "days run away like wild horses over the hills…"as he has moved on to heavenly pastures. Adios Joe.

JAYNE LYN STAHL is a widely published poet, and member of PEN American Center. Her new book, **Riding with Destiny**, is available from *NYQ Books*, a subsidy of *The New York Quarterly*. http://www.nyqbooks.org/title/ridingwithdestiny

WILLIAM TAYLOR JR. lives and writes in the Tenderloin neighborhood of San Francisco. His poems and stories have been widely published in the independent press in publications including *Poesy, The Chiron Review* and *The New York Quarterly*. His latest collection of poetry, **The Hunger Season**, was released by *Sunnyoutside* in 2009. **An Age of Monsters**, his first collection of short fiction, is forthcoming from *Epic Rites Press*.

MARK TERRILL's writings and translations have appeared in over 500 literary journals and anthologies worldwide, a dozen chapbooks, several broadsides and three full-length collections, including **Kid with Gray Eyes** (*Cedar Hill Books*) and **Bread & Fish (The Figures)**. A native Californian and ex-merchant seaman, he currently lives on the grounds of a former shipyard near Hamburg, Germany, where he's worked as a welder, road manager for rock bands, cook and postal worker.

ALEXANDRE THILTGES is the author of **Bukowski ou les Contes de la Violence Ordinaire**, *Paris: L'Harmattan*, 2006.

G. MURRAY THOMAS writes poetry, fiction, political commentary, literary and music criticism, and anything else that comes into his fool head. His new book of poetry, **My Kidney Just Arrived**, was published by *Tebot Bach* (Huntington Beach, CA) in early 2011. It contains poems dealing with Thomas' experiences on dialysis and his kidney transplant in April, 2010.

MICHAEL N. THOMPSON is the author of **Dancing Inside The Mouth Of Madness** and **This Hollow Pierces**. He has also been published in numerous literary journals. After nearly 20 years in Los Angeles barely surviving the death of hair metal, numerous riots and the Northridge earthquake, Michael lives in San Francisco where he cheers relentlessly for his beloved 49ers and Giants.

LAWRENCE WELSH was born and raised in South Central Los Angeles. Welsh first hitchhiked to New Mexico and Texas in 1989. Five years later, he moved to El Paso, where he still lives. A first generation Irish American and former award-winning journalist, Welsh has published eight books of poetry, including **Begging for Vultures: New and Selected Poems, 1994-2009** (*University of New Mexico Press*, 2011). A winner of the Bardsong Press Celtic Voice Writing Award in Poetry, Welsh is an associate professor of English at El Paso Community College.

LINDSAY WILSON an English professor at Truckee Meadows Community College, has published four chapbooks, has been named a finalist for the Philip Levine Prize, and has poetry forthcoming, or published in, *Salamander, The Portland Review, The New York Quarterly, The Clackamas Literary Review*, and *Verse Daily* among others.

A.D. WINANS is a native San Francisco poet and writer. He is the author of 53 books and chapbooks of poetry and prose. His work has been translated into eight languages.. In 2002 a song poem of his was performed at Alice Tully Hall, NYC. In 2006 PEN National awarded him a Josephine Miles Award for excellence in literature. In 2009 he was given a PEN Oakland Lifetime Achievement Award. In 2010, *BOS Press* published a book of his Selected Poems, **Drowning Like Li Po in a River of Red Wine**.

F.N. WRIGHT was born & raised in South Central Illinois. He left home at 16 & at 17 enlisted in the Navy. He is a Vietnam veteran. He is happily divorced & currently lives in a small trailer somewhere in the mountains of Southern Calif. He owns two Harleys & a souped up 1869 El Camino.

Since 1970 JOHN YAMRUS has published 2 novels, 18 volumes of poetry and has had more than 1,300 poems published in magazines around the world. Selections of his poetry have been taught at both the high school and university level and been translated into several languages including Spanish, Swedish, French, Italian, Japanese and Romanian. His latest book is **Can't Stop Now**.

ABOUT THE LUMMOX PRESS

LUMMOX Press was created in 1994 by RD Armstrong. It began as a self-publishing/DIY imprint for poetry by RD. Several chapbooks were published and in late 1995 LUMMOX began publishing the *LUMMOX Journal*, a monthly small/underground press lit-arts mag. Available primarily by subscription, the *LJ* continued its exploration of the "creative process" until its demise as a print mag in 2006. It was hailed as one of the best monthlies in the small press by John Berbrich and Todd Moore.

In 1998, LUMMOX began publishing the Little Red Book series, and continues to do so today. To date there are some 60 titles in the series and a collection of poems from the first decade of the series has been published under the title, **The Long Way Home** (2009); it's a great way to explore the series.

Together with Chris Yeseta (Layout and Art Direction since 1997), RD continues to publish books that are both striking in their looks as well as their content...published because of the merit of the work, not the fame of the author. That's why there are so many first full-length collections in the roster (look for the *).

The following books are available directly from the LUMMOX Press via its website: **www.lummoxpress.com** or at LUMMOX, c/o PO Box 5301, San Pedro, CA 90733. There are also E-Book (PDF) versions of most titles available. Most of these titles are available through other book sellers online, as well.

The Wren Notebook by Rick Smith (2000)

Last Call: The Legacy of Charles Bukowski
    edited by RD Armstrong (2004)

On/Off the Beaten Path by RD Armstrong (2008)

Fire and Rain—Selected Poems 1993-2007 Volumes 1&2
    by RD Armstrong (2008)*

El Pagano and Other Twisted Tales by RD Armstrong
(short stories—2008)*
New and Selected Poems by John Yamrus (2009)
The Riddle of the Wooden Gun by Todd Moore (2009)
Sea Trails by Pris Campbell (2009)
**Down This Crooked Road—Modern Poetry from
the Road Less Traveled** edited by RD Armstrong and
William Taylor, Jr. (2009)
The Long Way Home edited by RD Armstrong (2009)
Drive By by John Bennett (2010)
Modest Aspirations by Gerald Locklin & Beth Wilson (2010)
Steel Valley by Michael Adams (2010)*
Hard Landing by Rick Smith (2010)
A Love Letter to Darwin by Jane Crown (2010)*
E/OR—Living Amongst the Mangled by RD Armstrong (2010)
Ginger, Lily & Sweet Fire by H. Lamar Thomas (2010)*
Whose Cries Are Not Music by Linda Benninghoff (2011)*
Dog Whistle Politics by Michael Paul (2011)*
What Looks Like an Elephant by Edward Nudleman (2011)*
Working the Wreckage of the American Poem
edited by RD Armstrong (2011)
Living Among the Mangled (revised) by RD Armstrong,
special edition, (2011)
The Accidental Navigator by Henry Denander (2011)
Catalina by Laurie Soriano (2011)*
Born To Be Blue by Tony Moffeitt (2011)

www.ingramcontent.com/pod-product-compliance
Lightning Source LLC
Chambersburg PA
CBHW070039030726
47506CB00003B/803